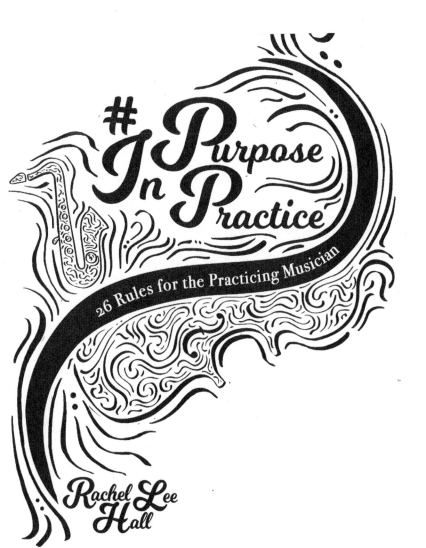

#In Purpose In Practice

26 Rules for the Practicing Musician

Rachel Lee Hall

Published by CrossRhythm Press
P.O Box 12401, Roanoke, VA 24025

ISBN: 978-1-7346271-1-4

Library of Congress Control Number: 2020902805

Printed in the U.S.A.

Table of Contents

Purpose In Practice

26 Rules for the Practicing Musician

Introduction

I started my practicing career at the tender age of six. It's hard to believe that twenty years have passed! At twenty-six years old, I find that my outlook on practicing has been shaped and challenged by an untold number of people and experiences. There is so much to share about what I have learned in my journey. What follows are twenty-six rules for practice—one rule for each year of my life—that have shaped me in life-transforming ways.

Although I write from the perspective of a harpist and occasional violinist, every chapter is filled with practical tools that any musician can incorporate both inside and outside their practice room. It doesn't matter if you play a harp or a piano or a flute or a hurdy-gurdy. If your goal is to improve your practicing, this book is for you.

There are many ways to use this book. A step-by-step guide to practicing well, this book is designed to go hand-in-hand with the Purpose in Practice Journal. The 6-month practice journal is a fun way to put into practice all the techniques you will find in this book. If you are using them together, feel free to read one chapter of this book per week as you work through your practice journal, implementing what you learn into your daily practicing. You can also use this book as a resource by flipping to whatever topic you are most interested in, or read it cover-to-cover for the full experience.

None of this book could have been written without the help of countless dedicated individuals. Though I can't possibly thank everyone who has shaped me, there are a few to whom I specifically want to express my gratitude: My parents, Steve and Vicki Hall, for everything they have taught me about a purposeful life. My older brother Jared, for exhibiting outstanding talent and diligence through every stage of this project. My younger brother Justin, for modeling excellence and maturity in everything that he does, and for his thoughtful guidance and advice. My boyfriend Jeremy, for his unwavering support and encouragement. My harp teachers, Anastasia Jellison and Yolanda Kondonassis, who have both proven to be outstanding teachers, mentors, and friends. Ms. Kondonassis, for her invaluable contributions to this book, as well as the wonderful contributions of Richard Weiss, Alan Bise, Brittany Lasch, Beomjae Kim, and Simone Dinnerstein. And my Instagram community, who continues to build me up and believe in me. I am grateful to you all.

As its title betrays, this book is all about finding purpose in your practice sessions. You may find, however, that many of these rules extend outside of your practice room as well. My greatest hope for this book is that it renews in you a sense of purpose that reaches far beyond the practice room into every aspect of your life journey.

Happy practicing!

Rachel Lee Hall

S.D.G.

Be Willing To Do Whatever It Takes

"Belief influences action,
and action influences belief."

— *Glenn Cunningham*

I t was a cold, bitter morning when the little Kansas schoolhouse erupted into flames. Earlier, seven-year-old Glenn Cunningham and his brother had arrived to warm up the room for school, and no one could have known that the can of kerosene had been accidentally refilled with gasoline. When his brother poured it over the hot coals, an explosion erupted which enveloped the schoolhouse in flames—and Glenn and his brother were trapped inside.

That morning in February of 1917 changed Glenn's life forever. His brother perished from the fire, and doctors told his mother that *if* Glenn survived, he most certainly would never walk again. The burns on his legs were too severe, having eaten away the flesh on his knees and shins, leaving him without toes on his left foot. The doctors strongly advised amputation so the infection wouldn't spread. His mother refused. That day, Glenn made what he would come to describe as one of the biggest decisions of his life: Against all odds, he decided that he would walk again one day.

Glenn took his first unassisted steps on Christmas Eve of that year. It had taken months of excruciating practice throughout the year, relearning how to stand and holding on to chairs or walls to take a step or two. Although every step was a jolt of shooting pain, Glenn knew that he needed to push through the pain in order to prove the doctors wrong. He kept practicing. Eventually, Glenn realized that it was a little less painful to run rather than walk, so he started to run everywhere. Through sheer determination, Glenn ran his way to winning his first race at age twelve. But he didn't stop there: He went on to compete and win prestigious awards in college, and he went to the Olympics twice, winning a silver medal in 1936. He set three world records and was an international sensation. People called him "the strongest miler to ever step on track."

A one-track mind

Glenn Cunningham not only defied the odds and learned to walk again, but his persistence led him to become one of the best runners in the world. This miraculous miler would have surpassed everyone's expectations if he had simply walked those few steps on Christmas Eve, but instead his continued determination allowed him to become one of the most amazing runners of all time. How could a small-town Kansas young-ster overcome so much and achieve such great things? How could a boy so grievously injured become a man who set world records and inspired millions of people?

He was willing to do whatever it took.

No matter how much discouragement he felt or how much pain he had to endure, seven-year-old Glenn Cunningham had a one-track mind. His purpose in life was to walk again, and that purpose fueled him to do whatever it took. Hard work, day in and day out, no matter the pain, Glenn pushed for the goal and he was rewarded for it in the end.

> *"How could a boy so grievously injured become a man who set world records and inspired millions of people? He was willing to do whatever it took."*

What is your pur-pose? Why do you do what you do? If you want to be successful, this is the first place to start. If you don't have a purpose you won't have a steady will to achieve. But if there is a pur-pose you believe in, you'll give your life to it, be willing to suffer for it, and nothing will stand in your way.

This book is all about purpose and practice. You can't have one without the other. Yes, you need to prac-tice hard to be great. But your practice will all be in vain unless you have a purpose for why you do it. And not just any purpose: It has to be a bold, brave one, one you believe in—one for which you might lay down your life.

If you have a purpose like that, hard work seems like a meager sacrifice.

This book is primarily for practicing musicians, but the rule applies to anyone, whether they are a musician or engineer or nurse or philanthropist or janitor. No matter your calling, you must first find a purpose worth living for. Once you have it, put that purpose into practice. Be willing to do whatever it takes to fulfill your calling.

Purpose in practice

Practicing becomes meaningful when you notice that it is slowly helping you to reach your biggest goals. Here are a few helpful steps to start putting your purpose into practice:

Make sure your purpose is worth it. A purpose that only accumulates selfish benefits is shallow. It reaches only one person, when potentially billions of people could be affected. Make a stand for a worthy purpose. As Glenn Cunningham often said, "If you don't stand for something, you'll fall for anything." When you weigh what your purpose is, ask yourself some deep questions. *Why do I do what I do? How can I influence and affect others with my talent and ambitions? Can I find a life purpose that is greater than myself?*

Count the cost. In order to accomplish your biggest goals, you will need to know what it will take to get there. Take a moment to write down your mission statement: at the end of your life, what accomplishment would satisfy you? What would make you feel like you had fulfilled your life mission? Under your mission statement, write down what you think it will take for you to get there. Then ask yourself these questions: How hard will you have to work? What might be some consequences of this pursuit? What will you have to give up to accomplish this mission? *Is it worth it?* But also count the cost of *not* pursuing your purpose. What might be some consequences of not pursuing this goal? What would you give up in pursuing other things instead? *Is it worth the sacrifice?* Counting the cost is essential to realizing whether you believe in your purpose enough.

Be stick-to-itive. Thomas Edison once said, "The three great essentials to achieve anything worthwhile are, first, hard work; second, stick-to-itiveness; third, common sense." In other words, be patient and persistent. Realize that reaching your goals won't happen overnight. Instead, it will require relentless hard work every day. Don't give up on your plan. Stick to it, be persistent, and watch yourself get closer and closer to the finish line.

Don't procrastinate. Putting off till tomorrow what could be done today might work for a high school student cramming for an exam. But with regard to one's life purpose, there is no place for procrastination. Only if you are all in will you do whatever it takes. You will realize it will take constant, relentless, committed, persistent work. You will not put it off. You will be excited to work toward that goal every day.

Pursue excellence. Don't settle for mediocrity. Commit to being absolutely the best you can possibly be. Expect more of yourself and then accomplish it! As Cunningham often said, "I'd rather be dead than be mediocre." If your purpose is worth living for, it is also worthy of your all—and that includes the pursuit of excellence in all that you do.

Use a practice journal. The Purpose In Practice Journal, the companion to this handbook, helps you achieve your biggest musical and personal goals. Use it to better organize yourself, track your progress, jot down new goals, analyze the data—all while you move towards more fruitful and efficient practice sessions.

Don't fear the failure (or success). Many times we choke on our biggest goals and dreams because we fear failure. Sometimes we choke because we fear success. Both can be scary: one might bring shame and the other responsibility. But fearing failure or success will only stifle your potential. You have been given some unique talents and gifts and you have an obligation to use them as best as you can. As Cunningham said, "Act as if it were impossible to fail." Don't let fear hinder you from reaching your biggest potential.

Whatever it takes

Glenn Cunningham was willing to do whatever it took to achieve great success in life. But his greatest success happened after he retired from running. Later in life, Glenn and his wife Ruth used their fame and wealth to make a big difference: fueled by the purpose they found in their Christian faith, Glenn and Ruth started the Glenn Cunningham Youth Ranch in Kansas, which grew to help more than ten-thousand underprivileged children find true purpose, meaning, and hope in the world.

It's amazing how many people were impacted simply by the determination of a seven-year-old. Next time you feel lacking in motivation or purpose, think of little Glenn Cunningham, who pushed through pain and hardship and ran to victory. He did whatever it took to fulfill his purpose. What is hindering you?

Review Questions

Question No. 1

Spend some time in contemplation. Why are you pursuing music? What is your greater purpose?

Question No. 2

What are one or two things you can do today that will get you one step closer to fulfilling your greater purpose?

Question No. 3

How do you think having a greater purpose will make you accomplish better things in the practice room?

≈ 2 ≈

Objectives
Make Effective

"The greatest adventure is what lies ahead.
Today and tomorrow are yet to be said.
The chances, the changes are all yours to make.
The mold of your life is in your hands to break."

— *J.R.R. Tolkien*

"Practice makes perfect," so they say. But that statement isn't exactly true. True perfection can be sought after but never quite achieved. Your piece can be almost perfect, but there is always a higher standard, there are always improvements to be made. That's why a famous artist once said, "An artist never finishes his work, he merely abandons it." Perfection may never be quite achievable in its fullest sense, but it is still a theoretical possibility. If we think of perfection in this way, it becomes a target to aim at. Though we may never hit the bullseye, higher levels of perfection can still be sought after and achieved. This kind of perfection is a standard by which to measure your efforts, and in this sense perfection is a matter of degrees.

Even if we could achieve complete perfection in our playing, it wouldn't be just any practice that would make it work. Only a certain type of practicing would make perfect. Through my experience and study of the practice session, I have boiled it down to two things. There are two magic skills a person can cultivate to achieve the right kind of practice that leads to higher levels of perfection: goal setting and efficiency. This chapter will consider the first: how to think about your practice sessions objectively in order to set the right goals for yourself. In the next chapter, we will discuss how to make the most of your time by practicing efficiently in order to accomplish those goals.

Goal setting

Setting goals is a valuable skill for any person, in any setting and in any stage of life. Are you a student? You need to set goals so you can study enough, get good grades, make it into your dream schools, and achieve the career you want. Are you a professional? You need to set goals to get to the next level in your career, maintain good family/work balance, and stay motivated in a workplace that might encourage burnout. No matter where you are in life, goal setting will get you farther, faster. It will help organize in your mind what you really want in life. And it will allow you to chip away at whatever obstacle lies between you and accomplishing your goals.

As musicians, we must take time to set both short-term and long-term goals in this chapter. I have provided below some advice for how you can set goals for yourself every day, week, month, and year. But before we get there, it is important to set some tentative long-term game-plans for 5 years from now and even at the end of your life. In order to best accomplish your goals, you must first zoom out and think big-picture.

Think long-term

Is it really necessary to think big-picture? Will this really inform our practice sessions? My conservatory harp teacher, Yolanda Kondonassis, seems to think so. "The concept is rather simple. You need to have a goal and plan to inform your daily work strategy or your practice will feel random and largely unfocused," she says. "Auditions, competitions, and performances are great ways to frame your goal-setting, but you always need to have a bigger picture and purpose in mind. What do you plan to do in order to leave your field, your community, your audiences, your students in a better position or mindset than you found them? That is always a good question to get your thinking started."

It all goes back to the question we posed before,

> *"You need to have a goal and plan to inform your daily work strategy or your practice will feel random and largely unfocused."*
>
> *—Yolanda Kondonassis*

"What is your purpose?" If you live to be a hundred, what would you need to accomplish in order to say, "I have lived my life to the fullest?" What regrets might you have? What would you wish to have spent more time on? This goes further than you and your music. Think about what you want in terms of career, family, service, faith, friends. Every now and then, think about this to gain perspective on what you value the most. Don't be afraid to think big here—this is your time to dream. How do you want to change the world—or at least your little corner of the world—with your life? If you could accomplish anything at all, what would it be?

When you get a clear picture of the above, make a five-year plan to better strategize how to accomplish it. Would your biggest musical goal be to eventually set up a music academy or summer festival? Work that into your five-year plan—how far can you get into accomplishing that in five years' time? Do you want to get an orchestra job or be a touring soloist? Research the ways you can take steps toward that goal. Do you need to apply for competitions, get with a specific teacher who can help you, or prepare for auditions? Analyze what it will take to get there and sketch it out in your five-year plan. You can accomplish a whole lot in five years, but it goes by at lightning speed. In order to accomplish the most, you'll need to make a plan.

Next, plan out your year, and each month of your year, based on your 5-year plan. How can you inch a little closer to your goals by taking it a month at a time? Here are a few monthly goal ideas:

- *Commit to consistent, daily practice (6 days per week).*
- *Learn a new piece in one month!*
- *Schedule a recital for the end of the month.*
- *Commit to memorizing a piece.*
- *Pick a technique you would like to master by the end of the month.*
- *Complete one medium-sized goal that would get you closer to accomplishing your big-picture goal, like applying for a competition or festival, researching and compiling your top five colleges lists, scheduling and learning required repertoire for upcoming auditions, or making a business plan.*
- *Commit to mental growth by maintaining better self-talk.*

In order to have focused and meaningful practice sessions, think long-term. Plan to live your life in order to be able to say at the end, "I couldn't have done anything better: I am satisfied."

Think short-term

This is where you can get specific. For short-term goals, I highly recommend using a practice journal. This will keep you organized and on course, and you will also have a visible and tangible way of tracking your progress and growth. The Purpose In Practice Journal is designed for this very purpose: to help you accomplish your short-term goals through a six month period.

First, think about your week in full. Be specific: what do you need to accomplish this week? Keep in mind the homework your private teacher gives you, or the orchestra music you have to learn, as well as your own personal goals. Write everything down in your practice journal. Here is what my list of weekly goals might look like:

- *Learn all of Hindemith Sonata*
- *Focus on a more open hand position*
- *Warm-up every day*
- *Go live on Instagram at the end of the week to showcase my progress*
- *Make dynamic and expressive decisions in Debussy*
- *Put pedals and fingerings in for orchestra music*
- *Decide on church music for Sunday*

Setting these goals at the beginning of the week will give you a better idea of what you need to accomplish. It will also ease your mind when you write them all down because your goals will seem more feasible on paper than floating around in your head.

With your week plan in mind, what do you need to accomplish today? This is where you can be really specific. The trick is making daily goals that are just enough of a stretch and challenge, while still being realistic. It can be frustrating if you make goals too unrealistic to finish. Start with what you know is attainable, and then stretch yourself by adding maybe one or two extra things for a special challenge. Here is a sample list of my daily practice goals:

- *Warmup with Kondonassis' Advanced Warmup. Focus on strong right-hand thumb*
- *Hindemith 1st movement: learn notes, first page only*
- *2nd movement, decide on fingering at beginning*
- *Get 3rd movement up to Eighth Note = 140 using #3xperfectly rule*
- *Write in markings for 4 pages of orchestra music*
- *Debussy: Decide on expression and dynamics for first sixteen bars*

Some musicians work better with very specific goals, and some work better with very broad ones. The most important thing is to stay your course. "I tend to be a rather specific goal-setter, with daily, weekly and yearly priorities," says Ms. Kondonassis. "However, some people do better with a larger and less specific arc. The most important thing is to set goals and make sure you keep the promises you make to yourself."

Whether they are broad or specific, consistent and methodical goal-setting will take you far. It might require some time to think long term, but it takes a few minutes to set daily goals for yourself in the practice room. When seeking to achieve higher levels of perfection, it helps to have a plan. And having a plan is the first step to efficient practicing.

Review Questions

Question No. 1

Why is goal-setting an important part of your journey as a musician?

Question No. 2

Take a moment to ponder your long-term goals. What would you need to accomplish in order to say, "I lived my life to my fullest?" Don't be afraid to think big: If you could accomplish anything at all, what would it be?

Question No. 3

How can you scaffold that long-term goal into a five-year plan? What can you do in five years that moves you one or two steps closer to accomplishing that life-goal?

Question No. 4

How does that five-year plan affect you this month? Write down a few monthly goals that will push you toward achieving your five-year goals.

Question No. 5

Next, think short-term. What do you need to accomplish this week? Write all of this down in your practice journal.

Question No. 6

Based on your goals for the week, what do you need to accomplish today? Use your practice journal to organize your thoughts and track your progress.

≈ 3 ≥

Practice As Little As Necessary

*"The successful warrior is the average man,
with laser-like focus."*

—*Bruce Lee*

W hen students ask cellist Richard Weiss how much they should practice, his answer is more than a little counterintuitive. "Practice as little as necessary," he says. This consummate cello pedagogue and associate principal cellist of the Cleveland Orchestra has much to offer by way of practice advice, and a good deal of it is wrapped up in this phrase. "The answer could be *as much as possible*," Weiss says. "However, my response is *as little as necessary* because it is the quality, not the quantity of work that matters."

The idea is this: if you give thought to the most efficient ways to practice, you can cut out a lot of wasted minutes, even hours, of practice time. Shorter, focused sessions of the best quality are more important and effective than aimless hours in a practice room.

Richard Weiss believes this idea in part because of the demands of his orchestra job. As a member of the Cleveland Orchestra, he holds a 52-week contract with different programs and multiple concerts each week. Weiss has learned to value efficient practice while preparing the vast repertoire that his position requires. "I practice these passages...with the goal of making ZERO mistakes in the first rehearsal," he says. "In order to learn new repertoire quickly, practice sessions need to be focused, thoughtful and patient. Within a few hours each day, great progress can be achieved."

> *"My response is as little as necessary because it is the quality, not the quantity of work that matters."*
>
> *—Richard Weiss*

What are the secrets to efficient practicing? Richard Weiss says the biggest secret is taking things slowly: "The art of slow-motion practicing is critical to achieving virtuosity," he says. "Of course, scales and études should be worked on with the same devotion to beauty of tone and precision that is required for solo repertoire." In addition, he offers these practice suggestions which are geared toward efficiency:

1. ALWAYS pause a few seconds between attempts at a tricky spot. Never rush to repeat a mistake. If an attempt is unsuccessful, give your brain a moment to recalculate. If an attempt is successful, a pause gives you time to reflect on and remember what went well so it can be learned and repeated.

2. ALWAYS choose a spot in the music to practice that is just before an obstacle. Starting over at the beginning of a passage is a waste of time. To efficiently learn a long, difficult passage, begin practicing the last measure, then the previous, and keep backing up further each time. This plan helps you build endurance and greatly increases the likelihood of getting through to the end without breaking down.

3. REMEMBER to sing a melodic passage before playing it. This helps to discover both natural phrasing and dramatic character. Engaging your breath also keeps your playing from feeling and sounding mechanical.

4. ALWAYS take care to avoid a negative facial expression. A furrowed brow in a challenging passage is a reaction which induces tension, and reduces your confidence for the next attempt. Replace this negative habit with a positive raising of the eyebrows which sets up a feeling of expected success.

5. ALWAYS consider a challenging passage as a puzzle to be solved. Like an art object, it can be viewed from several different angles until its secrets are revealed. This is the creative aspect of practicing that can actually be fun!

If you keep these things in mind like Richard Weiss and his students, you will be well on your way to mastering the art of efficient practicing.

How much is "as little as necessary?"

"So," you might ask, "I shouldn't have a minimum amount of practice time each day?" The answer is no, on the surface. The more important issue is that you reach all your goals for the day. That being said, if you find that you are accomplishing all your goals in a short amount of time every day, you may want to reevaluate your goals. With focused, efficient practicing, you will find that you are able to accomplish more in a day, so you may be able to make higher goals for yourself. I have found this chart to be a good rule of thumb:

	MINIMUM practice time to reach goals:
Beginner	30 minutes
Intermediate	1 hour
Serious Intermediate/ Advanced	2 hours

The chart should be more of a guideline than a rule. Some days your goals may be met in only thirty minutes and some days it may require eight hours! You should give yourself whatever leeway and flexibility your goals might require. But if you find that you, as a serious or advanced musician, are meeting your goals in less than 2 hours on average per day, you may need to set higher goals for yourself. The idea is to use all of your time to your best advantage. Focused practice can be liberating because it gives you more time to get your work done, ultimately resulting in more goals being accomplished faster.

You shouldn't be surprised, however, to find that intense, focused practice makes you more tired than longer, unfocused sessions might. Be sure to plan ahead for this.

"Quality is more important than quantity."

"Productive practicing requires intense concentration, so you should take a break each hour (perhaps 5-10 minutes)," Richard Weiss suggests. "It is possible to build endurance for long sessions of many hours, but you must be careful to avoid both physical and mental overexertion." Again, remember that quality is more important than quantity. Always be sure to implement good technique while practicing and never practice longer than is physically healthy. Some musicians, such as brass players are limited in the amount of time they can safely practice to avoid injury. Always consult a teacher or mentor when working out the perfect amount of practice time for your personal needs. Personally, I find that 3-4 hours of intense, focused, efficient practicing is about all my brain can handle in one day. After four hours of intense work, my ability for efficiency becomes less effective. Because of this, if I think that my goals will require me to practice more than four hours that day, I save the least brain-taxing work for the end. This is a personal discovery that works well for my brain and my instrument. But I would encourage you to do some exploration and experimentation to discover what works for you.

Rather than the common phrase, "practice makes perfect," consider revising your motto to "efficient makes proficient." As you learn to invest in more thoughtful, efficient practice, you will find that you have more time to rest, rejuvenate, and ultimately reach even higher and more ambitious goals for yourself. And, like Richard Weiss and his entourage of cello students, you will come to reap the benefits of practicing "as little as necessary."

Review Questions

Question No. 1

Why do you think that "Practice as little as necessary" is a more motivating prompt than "Practice as much as possible?"

Question No. 2

Why do you think that efficient practicing is important?

Question No. 3

What are some ways that you can eliminate wasted time in your practice room and take one or two steps towards more efficient practicing?

Question No. 4

Do you tend to accomplish your goals before the "minimum" time allotment in the practice chart? How might you modify your goals in order to achieve more?

≈ 4 ≈

Commit To Six Days Per Week (But Then Take A Day Off)

"Each morning sees some task begun,
Each evening sees it close;
Something attempted, something done,
Has earned a night's repose."

— Longfellow, The Village Blacksmith

You can usually group musicians into one of three categories. I noticed this during my time at the music conservatory, where I studied not only music, but also the habits of my peers. The first category is the group of people who are just a little bit lazy. They rely on their talent too much and tend to procrastinate to the day before their lessons or a week before their performances to achieve their goals. They may have been able to scoot by just fine during school but they never were *exceptional*—though they had the potential to be.

The second category is the group of people who never stop. I would hear about them but would never see them—they were always practicing. They never took time off, they never did anything fun. Their drive was admirable, but their need to be successful became obsessive and unhealthy—they burned out quickly and many of them didn't finish their degrees.

The third category is the group of people who learned how to mix just the right proportions of hard work and rest. These were the ones who truly succeeded in their degrees and their careers. As I observed my peers, I started to develop my own philosophy of what a successful work routine looks like, which included this controversial idea: *Commit to six days every week, but then take a day off.*

I feel a little counter-cultural in the classical music world when I encourage musicians to take a day off every week. It is a different rule than the more common one which you may have heard, "Only practice on the days that you eat." Why do I advocate for taking a day off? Because as much as I believe in the value of systematic, efficient, nose-to-the-grind, consistent work, I also have witnessed firsthand the value of rest. Our bodies are designed to require rest and in my experience, taking a full day to rest from practice does wonders—not only physically but mentally as well. It helps me with stress, keeps me from overthinking or obsessing about my playing, and puts things in perspective. And it helps me recharge and refresh my mind and body so that I will be better motivated to meet my goals at the start of the new week.

Here are four tips to experiencing a productive day off:

First, work hard for six days. This is a crucial part to the plan. If your six days of work are scattered, inconsistent and unproductive, then you really aren't working in such a way that rewarding yourself with rest is deserved. Be sure that your practice time is focused, goal-oriented, and consistent for six days. Commit to hard work first, then reward yourself with rest.

Plan out your schedule so you can afford to take a full day off. Afraid you don't have time to take a full day off? It just takes some planning and prioritizing. Olympic gymnast Simone Biles puts herself through rigorous training for 32 hours a week in addition to all her other activities, but she still can afford to carve out Sundays to rest. Even if you think you can't afford a full day off, you can probably afford a 24-hour period. Try getting all your practice done by 2pm one Saturday and then fast from practicing until 2pm on Sunday. Your body and mind will thank you.

"Go for a nature walk or a drive, write in a journal, have some tea, take a nap, spend time in solitary thought, take a bubble bath, read a book, listen to your favorite music."

Make sure your rest is purposeful. On your rest day, make sure you focus on real, intentional rest. Go for a nature walk or a drive, write in a journal, have some tea, take a nap, spend time in solitary thought, take a bubble bath, read a book, listen to your favorite music. Anything that helps you relax and just *be.* Many times we will do activities that aren't purposefully restful. These might include gaming, catching up on emails, binge-watching Netflix or scrolling through videos on Instagram. These are all rewarding activities in moderation, but hours of this on my rest day proves to be a waste of time and will be just as exhausting as a day of hard work! A day of rest should be just as purposeful as your days of hard work, so put some thought into how you can spend your day restoring, relaxing, and rejuvenating.

Recharge and get back in the game. Once your body and mind are restored and ready for your week ahead, get back to work! I am confident that you'll be better motivated to dig in deeper and maintain better focus as you work toward accomplishing your goals.

My first experience with this approach came at about eight years old when my Suzuki violin teacher, Mrs. Peterson, called me up on the phone one day.

"Hi Rachel! I'm calling to personally invite you to join my club!"

It was called the "6/7, 7/7 Club," and I felt that I must really be one special kid to have been included in her exclusive circle! All I had to do to be in the club was commit to practice six out of seven days and listen to music seven out of seven days. If I did this for the whole month I'd receive a special prize!

I joined the "6/7, 7/7 Club," and it took me a few years to realize that the real prize was not the Dairy Queen gift card at the end of the month but the gift of being introduced to such a powerful way of life so early.

Throughout my life, this approach has proven itself. I challenge you to try my method by committing for a month to hard work for six days and one day of rest. At the end of the month I am confident that you will find this approach rewarding in more ways than you might expect!

Review Questions

Question No. 1

What are some practical steps you can take towards maintaining more consistent practice time?

Question No. 2

How can you plan your week so that you can afford to take a day off from practicing?

Question No. 3

Why do you think rest is an important part of fulfilling your greater purpose?

Question No. 4

What types of activities can you plan on your rest day that make it purposeful?

≈ 5 ≈

Create
A Practice Haven

"We shape our dwellings,
and afterwards our dwellings shape us."

— *Winston Churchill*

I've practiced pretty much everywhere: hotel rooms, stairwells, bedrooms, bathrooms, closets, kitchens, laundry rooms, porches, restaurants, boutiques, and even mountain tops. At this point, I really believe that you can have a successful practice session *anywhere*, as long as you spend some time making it your own personal space. A practice space should be a haven to fly to, knowing and trusting that you'll always be able to fully focus and get things done.

Before you dive in to accomplish your goals, take a moment to make a haven of your practice room. You'll be spending a lot of time here, so it needs to invite focus, hard work, and clear thinking for the most productive practice day.

Where is the best place to practice?

Here are a few keys you can use to open the door into a great practice space, no matter where you might be.

Consider surface area. Make sure you have enough space to practice with your full range of motion. For me, I need to make sure that I don't bump anything with my hands when I raise off the harp quickly and that I can play my highest strings with my elbow up without hitting the wall. But I also try not to choose a space *too* big. For me, smaller spaces invite introspection, concentration, and focus, while larger spaces invite distractions. If you are practicing in a living room or large rehearsal room, consider mentally "roping off" a part of the room all to yourself. Oftentimes I orient my harp towards the corner of a room so that I'm facing the wall, forcing myself to look at nothing but my strings and the notes on the page.

Isolate. Ideally for me, a practice room would be away in some far-off cabin deep in the woods, where I see no one for days and I am left to the bliss of working at my own pace with zero distractions. Even though a log cabin may not be realistic, you can recreate the same type of isolation in your practice room. Make your practice room a true haven by distancing yourself from anything that might be distracting. Tell your friends you won't be able to respond to their texts for a couple hours. If you have roommates or family members who like to barge in, kindly explain to them that you'd be glad to talk to them after your practice session, but you really need to prioritize your work right now. Put your phone on airplane mode (more on this in the next chapter).

De-clutter. I think one of the biggest contributors to distraction is clutter. I'm not a perfectionist when it comes to organization, but I have noticed that the clutter of my mind is directly proportional to the clutter of my practice room. De-cluttering your practice space can do wonders for keeping your mind organized and focused, and by habitually keeping your practice haven tidy, you will condition your brain to think more logically and orderly.

Use Plenty of Light. Natural light is best, but any light will do. It's not fun at all to practice in the dark! If your practice room is too dark, invest in a floor lamp with a bright light bulb. Make sure your space is bright enough to clearly see your music and observe your technique. And much like the psychology in my previous point, if your practice haven has plenty of light your mood will likely be lighter, too.

Make it Yours. Spend some time making the space yours. Set up a little table next to you with a few essential practice tools: a metronome, practice journal, sticky notes, and a pencil. Print out some inspirational quotes to tape to the wall, or write notes of encouragement or reminders to yourself on sticky notes to place on the stand. Put one thing in the room that makes you happy or brightens the room. Light a candle, bring in fresh flowers, or throw a colorful, fuzzy rug on the floor.

Use a Mirror. Some of my biggest practice epiphanies came from looking at myself playing in a mirror. Ideally, a full-length mirror should be in every practice room. Use it to watch yourself at different angles and study your technique. What could you slightly change in order to have a better setup?

Bring snacks. A must. Fuel yourself, especially during long practice sessions! Some of my favorite practice snacks are bananas, mixed nuts, cheerios, granola bars, and chocolate on occasion (to reward myself for meeting goals). Bring anything that's quick and easy to snack on during a long practice session. Keep these on your side table too, along with a water bottle.

Dress the Part. I remember one occasion before my jury at school I was standing in the hallway applying lipstick when one of my professors walked up to attend the performance.

"I always play better with lipstick on," I said jokingly.

After I performed my jury, my professor quipped back, "I've got to get me some of that lipstick!"

All joking aside, the way you present yourself actually does have an impact on how you play. If you dress in a sloppy manner, you're telling yourself that your practice session, your instrument, and your goals really aren't that important. And you're ultimately telling yourself that *you're* not that important. Sloppy presentation makes for sloppy playing. Respect yourself a little more and dress the part. You don't have to dress up, but wear something to your practice session that you feel confident in—something you might wear to meet someone you respect. Because ultimately, you and your goals do deserve respect. Take a little time to dress the part. For me, a little lipstick goes a long way!

Next time you head into your practice room, see if you can implement some of these tricks to make your ordinary practice space a real haven for accomplishing your goals. Take some time before you start your practice session to create a space that is clean, inviting, ready for focus, and ultimately *yours*.

Review Questions

Question No. 1

What can you change or add to your current practice space that would invite more clarity, focus, and productivity?

Question No. 2

Jot down some ways that your surroundings might negatively affect your focus and productivity. How can you eliminate these distractions from your practice room?

Question No. 3

Think of attending a practice session like showing up for work. How might the way you dress affect the way you would respect yourself?

≋ 6 ≋

Put Your Phone
On Airplane Mode

"Concentrate all your thoughts upon the work at hand.
The sun's rays do not burn until brought to a focus."

— Alexander Graham Bell

Your phone is quite possibly your biggest enemy in the practice room. I could have crammed this point into the previous chapter, but it is so important that it deserves a chapter all to itself. The bottom line: phones can be a great asset to your practice time if you use them correctly. But if abused, phone use during practice sessions can be distracting at best and damaging at worst.

Don't get me wrong, I'm not against technology at all. Lest I come across that way, let's talk about all the benefits of smartphones to a practicing musician first. A smartphone can be a huge practice aid with all the apps it has to offer: Music dictionary apps, metronome apps (my favorite is Tempo Advance), tuner apps, Google translate, instant access to Wikipedia articles on every

composer, and the ability to listen to any of our repertoire with YouTube and Spotify at our fingertips. What
other era in life have practicers been able to prepare for
orchestra rehearsals by instantly pulling up the movement in question with one quick Google search and
playing along with the recording in realtime? Not to
mention the community building aspect of social media
platforms and the many ways musicians are connecting
all around the world to inspire, collaborate, and challenge each other. It really is a wonderful time to be alive.
The invention of the smartphone has given us innumer-
able assets which, if used properly, can be valuable tools
as we seek our biggest goals.

That being said, however, smartphones are absolutely just as dangerous as they are useful. For one thing,
increased cellphone use is contributing to anxiety and
stress. I recently learned of a new buzzword that refers
to people who struggle with cell phone addiction. The
word, "Nomophobia," (NO-MObile-PHOne-phoBIA) is
used to describe people who experience anxiety when
they are without their phone. The word was first used
in 2008 by the United Kingdom Post Office, when it was
discovered that approximately 53% of the UK popu-
lation admitted to feelings of uneasiness, anxiety, and
stress when their cell phone wasn't available to them.
How many of us would identify with these feelings of
uneasiness if we're being honest?

Mobile phones can have adverse effects on our
physical health as well. Some claim that mobile phone
addiction increases the likelihood of obesity. The dis-
torted neck position that is the trademark posture of the

mobile phone user can contribute to chronic musculo-skeletal neck pain. Our texting habits can cause injury too: I once knew a musician who struggled with tendinitis for months, thinking it had to do with a technique issue or practicing too much. Turns out, it was the way he was using his thumbs to text. Once he changed his texting habits, the tendinitis went away.

Finally, and perhaps most importantly, mobile phones are continually taking up more and more of our time. Studies have shown that a person touches their phone more than 2,617 times a day, with an average of 145 minutes spent in daily mobile phone usage. Let me do the math for you: That's more than *thirty-six DAYS* that an average person spends on their phone per year! How many of you could use thirty-six extra days in your year? How many times have you complained so far this year about not having enough time to accomplish your goals?

With these statistics in mind, what do you want to bet that your mobile phone might be hindering you in the practice room? I know personally the ways my phone usage has been a hindrance to me. I've devised a list of guidelines that have proven to be immensely helpful to me in this regard, and I invite you to follow them for a month and see if it improves your practice life—and your life in general!

> *"How many times have you complained so far this year about not having enough time to accomplish your goals?"*

Place your phone on airplane mode while practicing. Do you find it tempting to scroll through Instagram during your practice session? What if you just got rid of the temptation entirely by committing to put your phone in Airplane Mode whenever you're practicing? Placing your phone in Airplane Mode allows you to use any app that doesn't require WiFi or data. That means you can use your metronome for hours without ever having the temptation to scroll through Instagram! You should only ever allow yourself to take your phone off Airplane Mode *momentarily* during a practice session for two reasons:

- *To listen to your piece. You can plug in your headphones and play along, or study your score while listening.*

- *To look up relevant information, such as an expressive marking definition or lyric translation.*

Can you think of many other reasons why you would need WiFi to practice? As soon as you're finished listening or looking up information, turn your phone back to Airplane Mode. I strongly recommend this approach. Make a pact with yourself to commit for a month. It works wonders.

Limit phone usage throughout the day, too. Don't take your phone with you to use the restroom or eat meals. Leave it in the car if you're meeting a friend for coffee. Consider turning your phone off half an hour before bed and not turning it on until half an hour after you wake up. Instead, budget in time to use your phone every day as a reward for accomplishing your daily goals. This way, you can reap the benefits of having a smartphone without making it a dangerous distraction.

Modifying your mobile phone usage could be transformative! It could give you more peace of mind, concentration, focus, a greater sense of freedom, and strengthen your relationships. If every practicer placed their phone in Airplane Mode during all their practice sessions, it's hard to say how many virtuosos the world would produce! Give yourself the gift of an uninterrupted practice session by being more mindful of how you use your phone.

Review Questions

Question No. 1

What are some ways that using your phone in your practice session is helpful? What are some ways that phone use is unhelpful?

Question No. 2

How do you feel that modifying your phone usage in your practice room could benefit your overall productivity?

Question No. 3

What other areas of your life can you limit your phone usage? How might this affect you in a positive way?

≈ 7 ≈

Those Who Band Together
Stand Together

"Alone, we can do so little;
together, we can do so much"

— Helen Keller

You might have heard of the ancient African proverb which says, "It takes a village to raise a child." But did you know that it also takes a village to raise a musician? If you want to grow as a musician, it is neither healthy nor realistic to do it alone. You are going to need as much help as you can get! Band yourself to a community who will be willing to help you as you work towards becoming an even better musician.

Join a band

I don't mean *that* kind of band—the one your best friend's brother started in his parents' basement during high school (although that's somewhat on the right track). I'm talking about a band of people who are committed to similar goals. Banding yourself together with such a community helps you connect and bond in ways that give you lasting purpose and inspiration. Success is never an inside job. If you want to succeed, you need to have the humility to invite people to come alongside you in your journey.

Band aid

It's hard to quantify the value of banding yourself to a group of similarly motivated people. The right community can give you the right aid you need in your pursuits as a musician. Here are some perks to becoming part of a community:

Your community will keep you accountable. This is probably the most obvious perk. A group of people who care about you will hold you accountable. You should feel completely okay asking them to send you a text saying, "Hey, did you practice today?" Or set up some deadlines together: "Let's play our etudes for each other at the end of the week." Find a community that respects your goals and isn't afraid to hold you accountable to them.

Your community will inspire you. One of my favorite things about my presence on social media is how inspiring the Instagram music community can be! If I'm feeling unmotivated, all I have to do is scroll through the #PurposeInPractice hashtag and I'll soak up enough inspiration to last me the week! A community of ambitious people will inspire you to keep going, no matter how uphill the road might be.

Your community will give you healthy competition. In high school I was a member of my local youth orchestra, where I played not only harp, but also first violin. The string players had auditions every week for chair placement, and my two best violin buddies were my biggest competitors: it was Rachel, Sage and Daria vying for that concertmaster chair every week! I'm so thankful for the experience I had of weekly competition with my friends! It didn't become an aggressive or obsessive urge to compete and win—it was like a game for us. It was a way for us to find commonality in something, work at it together, and succeed together. No matter who eventually won the concertmaster spot for the performance, there was never jealousy—we were happy for each other as we mutually sought to be our best.

> *"It's hard to quantify the value of banding yourself to a group of similarly motivated people. The right community can give you the right aid you need in your pursuits as a musician."*

Your community will give you healthy criticism. A good community encourages you as you seek to improve in your playing (i.e., *That sounded great! You were* *phenomenal! Good job!*), but a *great* community gives you constructive criticism so that you can be better. Learn to have the humility to ask for advice and get some feedback, because no matter how much it might hurt your pride, nuggets of wisdom are far more valuable than lumps of empty praise.

Your community will give you perspective. Speaking of humility, the right community can keep you from becoming too self-focused or prideful (remember how this type of thinking makes your purposes shallow?). They'll help you realize your place in the world, "as good as the best and no better than the rest." They'll motivate you to gain some perspective on the things that truly matter in life and remind you of the real reasons why you do what you do. The right community gets you out of your own headspace and certainly your practice room, and propels you towards healthier mindsets and more significant goals.

> *"A good community encourages you as you seek to improve in your playing, but a great community gives you constructive criticism so that you can be better."*

Your community will keep things fun. A good community not only motivates and inspires you, it also helps you loosen up and take yourself less seriously!

Get together and have a jam session, or get a coffee and laugh about your worst performances ever. Collaborate on projects and perform together using your unique talents. Band together and unite in your love and passion for the arts!

Whether it's an Instagram community, an orchestra, your teacher's studio, or a local arts organization or music society, find a community that will help you grow into the musician you crave to be. And who knows? Maybe you'll also find that as you put down roots in that community, you will start helping others in their quests to become better artists, too. Those who band together stand together.

Review Questions

Question No. 1

What are the benefits of being part of a healthy community?

Question No. 2

How does your presence in your community help you grow?

Question No. 3

How can you pour into your community for the benefit of others?

≋ 8 ≋

You Are An
Athlete

"If you fail to prepare, you're prepared to fail."

— *Mark Spitz*

Have you ever imagined yourself as an Olympic athlete? Take a moment sometime to look up a few of today's biggest sports stars and athletes, and you may start to notice some patterns. All the greatest athletes take their goals so seriously that every moment matters. Their bodies are fine-tuned and daily routines are prioritized to the minute. Nutrition, rest, and recovery are all scheduled and considered just as important as their training.

Though you may not be as physically fit as an Olympian, the time you spend with your instrument taxes your body more than you might suspect. Start to think of yourself as an athlete and create a daily routine that prioritizes the care of your body as you work toward your biggest practice goals.

Here are some ways that considering yourself as an athlete will help you reach your goals:

Embrace the warmup

Any athlete will tell you the importance of a warmup before training. Warming up your muscles helps both your body and mind to be sharper and prepares you for anything you might encounter in your practice session. It may seem like a waste of time when you have so much to accomplish, but there is no telling just how valuable a good warmup can be for efficient practice. Here's what I've learned about warming up.

Slow warmups are better than fast warmups. Slow work wakes up your muscles and retrains them to cooperate with your mind. I strongly suggest starting a practice day with some slow scales and arpeggios while focusing on good form and technique. You can slowly increase your warmup tempo as your fingers and brain wake up.

Choose a warmup that aligns with your daily practice goals. If your biggest practice goal is to get better at trills, implement trills in your warmup. If you want to work on your bow distribution, choose a warmup that will force you to focus on bowing. If your goal for the day is breath control, warm up accordingly. Be purposeful about your warmup to get your mind focused on the task you most want to accomplish that day.

Make warmups out of your rep. By all means create warmups out of your current repertoire! You can do this by slowing down tricky, technical passages and Boot Camping them (more on this in Chapter 12) or by changing up the rhythms and accents. This is a great option when you don't think you have time for a warmup, because it makes your practice session extra efficient!

Take care to watch out for bad technique

This is essential. No matter how quickly you need to learn a piece, good technique and form is more important. Bad technique can lead to injury fast, which is the most crucial and obvious point. But the value of good technique goes beyond lack of injury. I am forever grateful for my first harp teacher, Anastasia Jellison, who insisted on building a solid foundation of good technique in my early years as a harpist. For me, this foundation means I have the freedom to accomplish anything and everything at my instrument! Like a fledgling who learns how to properly use its wings, if you learn proper technique you can soar. This freedom

> *"For me, this foundation means I have the freedom to accomplish anything and everything at my instrument!"*

requires a lot of foundational work and maintenance, so here are some guidelines that can help:

Keep a checklist of technical concerns. It helps to physically write out checklists of things you need to watch out for in a practice session. This will not only jog your memory but also give you more incentive to maintain good technique. For me, simply filling in a bubble with a check mark is incentive enough to accomplish the task in question!

Remember that everyone has an Achilles' heel. Everyone has that one thing that they need to always look out for when it comes to form and technique. For me, it's my right hand thumb. It's shorter than most and a little double jointed, so it tends to collapse and not sound as articulate as I would like. Since melodies are most often played with the right-hand thumb on the harp, this could be a huge disadvantage! But I choose to think of it as an advantage instead. If I'm constantly mindful about my "Achilles' heel," I'll give way more attention to that part of my technique than other harpists, so my right hand thumb can actually sound more perfected and articulate and stand out in a good way.

Don't relax your focus. Bad habits are usually formed from a collection of small, seemingly insignificant surrenders to relax one's vigilance. Don't ever allow yourself to say "just this once." Stomp out bad habits before they even start by committing to good technique every day.

Realize that good habits are formed with time. Learning good technique isn't going to happen overnight. Be patient, work slowly, and reward yourself for small victories! Soon you will be able to look back and see how far you've come.

Listen to your body

Most people don't realize just how taxing playing an instrument can be on the human body. Just as an athletes must care for themselves in order to be their best, so should you. Your body is so much more important than your practice session, instrument, or career.

Take practice breaks. Avoiding breaks during a long practice session will strain your mind as well as your body. A good rule of thumb is to take ten minutes every hour, or thirty minutes every hour and a half. Even if this can't be achieved, commit to leaving your practice space for at least five minutes every hour to stretch. You might be surprised by how refreshing and helpful this can be!

Hydrate. Bring your water bottle to every practice session. If you drink a full bottle of water per hour, you'll give yourself more incentive to leave your practice room for a practice break by filling it back up!

Fuel yourself with good nutrition. A friend of mine in college would often remind me, "Food is essential for life." That's obvious, isn't it? But all too often when I get busy I tend to forget to eat, skip meals, or grab something quick that isn't the healthiest choice. It's hard to quantify how beneficial good nutrition can be towards reaching your goals and achieving great practice.

Prioritize sleep. Ask any pro athlete about the most undervalued asset to training and they'll tell you "recovery" every time. Did you know that Lebron James sleeps for 12 hours a day — usually an average of 8-9 hours per night with a 3-hour afternoon nap? Studies show that getting adequate sleep helps basketball players perform with better speed, reaction time, and a 9% increase in shooting accuracy. Don't you think that getting enough sleep will help your playing accuracy, too? Rest is your most valuable asset, and yet today our culture glorifies how little we can sleep to function. Don't give in to that! It can take discipline to put your phone aside at night and make sure you get your 7-8 hours in, but that discipline is worth it. Many times, after a series of long, frustrating practice sessions, just putting your instrument away and getting an extra hour of sleep is more beneficial than practicing another hour into the night. This has proven to be the case for me on countless occasions.

> *"Just as athletes must care for themselves in order to be their best, so should you."*

Stretch and exercise regularly. Find stretches and exercises that complement the workout you are already getting with your instrument. For me, that means hiking or jogging and exercises that strengthen my core, neck, and hands. For you musicians who benefit from strong fingers, I strongly recommend using therapy putty for strengthening your muscles and joints. For every musician, I would emphasize building a strong core. I firmly believe that this is one of the secrets to avoiding many instrument-related injuries. A few sit-ups a day can go a long way!

Try to play with as little tension as possible. Tension is a harbinger of injury. Learn to spot the reasons you get tense at your instrument, and train yourself to relax and breathe even during the most technically difficult passages.

In the case of injury, don't be a "hero." If you are experiencing chronic pain related to your instrument (especially nerve or tendon pain), please stop practicing and go see a doctor. There are people in the classical music world that glorify powering through major injuries. But don't listen to these lies! There is no award given for massive injury. There is no glory in ruining your body. Oftentimes a doctor can diagnose and quickly treat a problem, and I have experienced the wonders of a few sessions of occupational therapy in the face of injury. Take advantage of these options! Use them to take care of the problem quickly so you can get back to work. As Lebron James says, "The body is the number one thing. It's the temple. We always listen to the body. If you don't listen to the body, it will fail you."

Though it takes some discipline, the combination of dozens of these small (or not-so-small) advantages can have a huge effect as you take your skills to the next level. "The one thing that's common to all successful people," says Michael Phelps, "they make a habit of doing things that unsuccessful people don't like to do." Start thinking of yourself as an athlete and see how far you can go in achieving your goals.

Review Questions

Question No. 1

In what ways is being a musician like being an athlete?

Question No. 2

Why are warmups important for musicians? How can you implement more purposeful and productive warmups into your practice sessions?

Question No. 3

Do you have an "Achilles' Heel" in your technique? What are one or two technique issues that you should always watch out for?

Question No. 4

As you practice, what are some ways that you can be more in tune to your body? In what ways can you prioritize your rest, nutrition, exercise, and relaxation like an athlete might?

≈ 9 ≈

Mindfulness
Is Key

"Only through focus can you do world class things,
no matter how capable you are."

— *Bill Gates*

When I asked concert pianist Simone Dinnerstein what she considered the most important rule for practicing, her response was "Being present." This internationally known performer has learned in the busyness of life how to relish each moment in the practice room and use every one to its fullest by practicing mindfully. "I spent many years wasting time practicing on autopilot, not being mindful," Dinnerstein says. But suddenly, when her son Adrian was born, she found she had much less time for practicing. "I had to make wise choices for how to most effectively use my time, and I realized that if I was truly alert and engaged I could achieve a lot more in a shorter period of time."

Like Richard Weiss and his discoveries of efficient practicing, Dinnerstein realized that being mindful in every moment of a practice session is the key to improvement. Giving every moment of your practice session your fullest attention will produce fruit that you have never seen before.

The danger of mindlessness

"If at first you don't succeed, try, try again" is a mantra we have heard since probably before we could walk. It speaks to the necessity of persistence and stick-to-itiveness to reach a goal, as well as the importance of repetition in order to master a skill. Success is achieved only through relentless, repetitive practice—through a series of trying and trying again, like a muscle that needs to be continually built up and exercised until it is strong.

But like a muscle which can be susceptible to injury, there are dangers to practice if it is mindless. If you are lifting weights without giving any thought to good technique and form, hours in the gym will prove to be ineffective at best and disastrous at worst. If you are using your equipment mindlessly, injury is sure to occur. Just like a workout with weights, practicing is a piece of equipment we can use to strengthen ourselves—but we have to do it with proper form and the right precautions. We must take care to exercise *mindful*, rather than *mindless*, practice.

> *"Like a muscle which can be susceptible to injury, there are dangers to practice if it is mindless."*

Practice mindfully

Here are some ways you can be more present in your practice room:

Learn how to exercise mindful repetition. In your practice session you will realize that repetition is necessary in order to learn your notes. But take care not to simply repeat whole passages over and over again with little thought to actually learning. Consider using the #3xperfectly rule: Commit to achieving higher degrees of perfection by playing the section three times perfectly before moving on to a new section or new tempo. That means three times without any slight slip-up, wrong note or fingering. If you mess up on the second try you have to go back to square one. This technique forces you to focus in, truly listen, and practice repetitively in a way that is mindful. It gives your brain the information necessary to store and organize the notes in your mind.

Isolate microsections. It may be counterintuitive, but isolating your music into microsections is the fastest way to learning notes. Most often when my students come to me saying they had trouble learning their assignment, it is because they tried to learn too much of it at once. Take a measure or less and dissect it. Practice one microsection at a time. Then, piece them together slowly and methodically (you can use the #3xperfectly rule as you do this!). This technique also works well when you're using your metronome or trying to memorize (I talk more about using this practice technique in chapters 13 and 18).

Get better at focusing. See if you can expand the amount of time you are able to focus every practice session. Do you find that you start to lose focus after 15 minutes? Work hard to stay focused that long, and the next session try to stay focused for 16. Consider other factors that might contribute to trouble focusing: are you sleeping enough? Getting the right nutrition? Are you practicing at the right time of day? The ideal time of day is different for everyone (for me, I focus best in the late afternoon), so experiment a bit to find out when the "golden hours" of practice time are for you.

When your mind wanders, switch it up. Simone Dinnerstein pays close attention to when she starts to lose focus and plans for it. "I try to work on the most difficult spots first, when I am the most alert," she says. "When my mind starts to wander, I change to practicing something entirely different. For instance, if I was working in a very detailed way on particularly challenging areas, I will rest that part of my brain by playing through an entire piece. Practicing performing an entire piece without stopping is quite different than honing in on a detailed problem." Be sure that you are taking breaks, too. If you've been practicing intensely for more than an hour, standing up for a 5-minute stretch break might be all your mind needs to get back in the game.

Be present

As you work towards being more present in your practice time, you might discover that you will come to enjoy it more and more. You'll find yourself engrossed in the music and experiencing joy in it in completely new ways. "The most interesting and exciting aspect of being a musician for me is getting inside the world of the music itself," Simone Dinnerstein says. "I love the process of delving into a score and trying to understand the different directions it can take." Be present. Relish every moment of your practice time. The more you work towards practicing mindfully, the more your music will come to life.

Review Questions

Question No. 1

How can mindful practice benefit you in the practice room?

Question No. 2

What is the #3xperfectly rule? Why is it effective?

Question No. 3

Why do you think practicing in microsections is an effective practice method?

Question No. 4

What are one or two ideas from this book that you can work on to improve your focus while practicing?

≈ 10 ≈

You Are Your Own Worst Critic

"I am hitting my head against the walls,
but the walls are giving way."

— *Gustav Mahler*

One of the highlights of my harp career so far was performing in the final round of the 2019 Ima Hogg Competition. I was playing the Ginastera Harp Concerto, and the final round was performed with the Houston Symphony Orchestra. I vividly remember the excitement of being backstage, moments away from my grand entrance. I didn't feel nervous in the least! All I felt was excitement. It was intermission, and from backstage I could see glimpses of faces in the audience. I felt a wave of gratitude for how kind everyone in Houston had been to me that week. These faces weren't stern or judgmental, but soft, happy, and just as excited as I was, anticipating what they would hear next. As I looked into the audience, I knew that I was ready. No matter what music critic or jury member was out there, it didn't matter. I had already been accepted by the worst music critic I knew—myself!

Have you ever wished you could have your teacher sit through all your practice sessions? How helpful would it be to have someone yell, "Don't rush!" or, "Elbow up!" every time you forgot? I often wished this growing up, until I realized that an even better option was to teach myself how to think and listen critically to my own playing. I knew my limits and my potential better than my teacher did. Teaching myself how to be my own worst critic helped me grow leaps and bounds in the practice room.

Embrace the job of worst critic

Give yourself the job description of being your own worst critic in the practice room. In other words, set the highest expectations for yourself. Use your ears to analyze your playing during your practice sessions. Is your tone pure? Is it even? Is the rhythm correct? Are you rushing? If you say, "maybe just a little bit, but it's probably good enough," the answer is *no!* "Good enough" should never be uttered by you—you are your own worst critic, after all, so expect more!

Of all the people in the world, you are the best expert on yourself. Use this knowledge to propel yourself forward in expecting bigger and better things. Complacency has no place in the job description of "Worst Critic"—you need to have higher expectations. Expect precision, excellence, and beauty. Expect consistency—it's not good enough if you can play the passage correctly every now and then, or even *most* of the time. If you have the expectation of playing it right every time, you'll put in the work to make sure that happens.

Use this to your advantage

Learning how to become your own worst critic can be a huge advantage to your development as a musician. First of all, expecting more of yourself will grow you in unimaginable ways. You can set bigger goals for yourself, challenge yourself more, and gain better precision and excellence in your playing. But you also will find, as I did, that it helps with performance anxiety, too. If you become your own worst critic, you have less to worry about on stage. You can tell yourself, as I did, that there isn't any critic more formidable in the audience than you, and you are going to be just fine.

Taking on the job of worst critic doesn't mean you can get away with being critical in a negative way, however—that's below your pay-grade. Don't allow any criticism that falls into the "negative self-talk" category. Never tell yourself you're stupid, a bad player, or that you *can't* do something (we'll talk about this in depth in the next chapter). There is only constructive criticism in this job description! Be critical and set high expectations only because you respect yourself enough to do so.

Learn how to turn off your worst critic

Being your own biggest critic will help you grow immensely as a musician. But when you get to a performance, you need to be able to turn your worst critic off. Your worst critic should be present in every practice session leading up to a performance, but once you have practiced your hardest and accomplished all that you can, he or she should declare that you are "worthy of performing" and then go away for a little while. Don't take your worst critic on stage, but leave him or her in the practice room. After all your hard work, your worst critic deserves a break—and you deserve to fully enjoy your performance without counting mistakes or worrying about any expectations

> "Don't take your worst critic on stage, but leave him or her in the practice room. After all your hard work, your worst critic deserves a break—and you deserve to fully enjoy your performance."

you should have. Later, you might be able to listen to a recording with your worst critic, or go back through your music and study things that happened during the performance. But for now, don't worry about making mistakes and just enjoy the moment. Your worst critic has given you permission to go out there, enjoy your performance, and shine.

Backstage at the Ima Hogg Competition finals, all of this flooded through my brain. I told myself I had practiced diligently, worked hard, done all that I could to be where I am at this moment. I left my worst critic backstage, took a deep breath, and made my entrance.

Performing that night was exhilarating and so much fun—and as it turns out, I won the gold medal! But as much as that prize meant to me, and as generous as it was, the real prize was being able to enjoy a moment like that in peace.

Learn the secret of becoming your own worst critic! Use this to your advantage, make sure it is always constructive, and learn how to turn it off when you need to. As you learn to expect more of yourself and listen to yourself more carefully, you will be excited to see how much you grow, not only as you improve in the practice room, but as you improve with performance anxiety as well. After all, there isn't any critic more formidable than yourself!

Review Questions

Question No. 1

Give yourself the job description of being your own biggest critic. How can you accumulate small advantages in the practice room in order to improve?

Question No. 2

Do you err towards being too hard on yourself or not hard enough? How does this affect your practice sessions?

Question No. 3

What are some ways you can be your own biggest critic while still maintaining a healthy view of yourself?

≋ 11 ≋

Can't
Is A Bad Word

"There is nothing difficult,
there are only new things, unaccustomed things."

— *Carlos Salzedo*

A practice session can reveal a lot about ourselves. Practicing requires a lot of patience—patience to learn notes, develop a good technique, gradually get a piece up to tempo, and let the music steep enough to get a sense of what we want to say with it. But practicing most of all requires patience with ourselves. In order to have a great practice session, we must commit to being our own biggest ally in the practice room. And that starts with vowing to never say the word "Can't."

"I'm so stupid! Why can't I get this right?"

I was a young teenager, trying to learn some new notes. Feeling the pressure of a time constraint, it seemed to me like I wasn't making any progress. As my dad walked by the music room, he heard me exclaim to myself in exasperation, "I'm so stupid! Why can't I get this right?"

He stopped and rather firmly told me to *never* say something like that to myself. I was a little surprised. "If you make a mistake, never tell yourself you're stupid. Never say you can't. Instead, say something like, *"Well, that wasn't like me. I'll do better next time."*

Growing up in the Hall household, words like *can't* and *stupid* weren't allowed. Of course we weren't allowed to tell other people they were stupid, but we weren't allowed to tell ourselves that, either. I'm thankful that I was taught early on the destructive nature of negative self-talk. I admit that in a moment of frustration it can be tempting to take out that anger on yourself with bad words. But negative self-talk is more harmful than you might realize. Think about every negative word you say to yourself as a punch in the stomach. Maybe you think you deserve it, but sooner or later it's going to bring you down—along with your expectations, productivity, ability, and joy. Negative self-talk is the easy route, but disciplining yourself to only tell yourself what is constructive and life-giving is what will bring the most good and progress in the long run.

Destroy negative self talk

Can't is a bad word. So are phrases like "I'm an idiot," "I'm so stupid," or "What's wrong with me?" Would you say any of these things to your best friend or your mom? You can expect a lot of yourself and give yourself constructive criticism without any of that negative self-talk. Respect yourself enough to tell yourself the things that build you up. Destroy negative self talk before it destroys you.

A practice haven is a really safe place to fail

Have you ever thought about this? You can take as many risks as you like in a practice room. It's just you and yourself in the mirror, after all. No one is listening, no one is watching. This is the place to experiment, try new things, and let yourself explore your instrument. It's the place to fix technical problems, slowly and patiently watching for progress. It's the place to try wild expressive ideas and then maybe decide against them. It's the place to learn and grow. And let's be honest: you're not going to get it right all of the time. Sometimes you'll fail. But don't get frustrated. Don't get exasperated. You're OK, because a practice haven is a really safe place to fail. You can only grow from there.

Never tell yourself something is difficult

I came to personally realize this while learning Renie's *Legende* at the harp. It's a lovely showpiece based on a story about a knight, a princess, and evil forest elves, and it was the most difficult piece I had learned to date. The hardest part was right in the middle of the piece: two whole pages of tremolos. This was the part in the legend where the elves come out and dance for the knight, attempting to bewitch him. The passage thus had to be completely light and completely even, while also allowing the melody to cut clear across all the filigree. Frankly, I was afraid of it. I treated it like my greatest enemy. I practiced slowly, did the #3xperfectly rule for microsections, and used my metronome. *I will beat this,* I told myself. But whenever I tried to play it at tempo, my hands failed me. *I couldn't do it.* And I was frustrated.

Finally, I realized that I had been thinking of this passage all wrong. I had been psyching myself out about the piece so much that my heart would jump whenever I turned the page to the tremolo section. It wasn't that I was denying my fear. I readily admitted I was afraid of it, and I had set out to beat it like a knight might challenge his foe to a duel—*to the death.* But it wasn't working, and finally, I realized why.

This piece wasn't my greatest enemy, I realized. In reality, it was a reliable friend. These notes were brilliantly composed, and they were a help, not a hindrance, in painting the picture I wanted to display for my audience. "No need to be so dramatic and fight to the death for a crushing victory, Rachel," said I to myself, "when you don't even have an enemy to fight." I started approaching it like I would approach a friend. I stopped thinking of it as difficult, and tried to

> *"This piece wasn't my greatest enemy, I realized. In reality, it was a reliable friend."*

smile and enjoy practicing it. I eventually taught myself to love that tremolo section. It took some doing, but once I did my hands relaxed and became nimble as elves, and the passage flowed as smoothly as I had always imagined.

Legende was one of the most transformative pieces for me to learn, not because I finally figured out how to play fast tremolos, but because of the deeper life lesson which will stick with me for the rest of my life. Obstacles aren't enemies to overcome, they're friends to help you grow. As the harpist Carlos Salzedo said, "There is nothing difficult; there are only new things, unaccustomed things." Once you stop telling yourself something is difficult, once you embrace it and commit to growing, you will come to realize that there is less to fear and more to love—not just in your practice room, but in every aspect of your life.

Review Questions

Question No. 1

Why is negative self-talk dangerous?

Question No. 2

What are the typical negative things you say to yourself? How can you learn to stop telling yourself those things?

Question No. 3

What are some seemingly impossible obstacles in your practice room? How can you think about them differently in order to overcome them?

≈ 12 ≈

Sign Up For
Boot Camp

"One must always practice slowly.
If you learn something slowly, you forget it slowly."

— *Itzhak Perlman*

Every prospective harp student at the Cleveland Institute of Music is forewarned: if you accept a place in Yolanda Kondonassis' studio, you are signing up for at least one semester of all-intensive Boot Camp. Just like a new recruit trains for the military through an intensive and fundamental training regimen, new harp recruits at CIM get ready for performance through intensive and fundamental training at the harp. Many of us didn't even learn real pieces for the first few weeks of freshman year. We went through Boot Camp instead—and it changed our lives.

What is Boot Camp? It's a practice method founded by Yolanda Kondonassis, designed to help musicians focus on the technical aspect of playing. "I coined the phrase 'Boot Camp' very early on in my teaching career

> *"I coined the phrase 'Boot Camp' very early on in my teaching career as a way of describing the practice of addressing the purely physical and fundamental elements of playing any passage"*
>
> —Yolanda Kondonassis

as a way of describing the practice of addressing the purely physical and fundamental elements of playing any passage," she says. Her philosophy is that before anything else happens, notes should first be scrutinized carefully, with the utmost attention on precision and technique. How do you do that? On the harp, it is achieved by practicing slowly and loudly. "Boot Camp practicing is usually most helpful at a slow speed and high volume in order to maximize the muscle control/muscle memory aspect of a given figure or passage," she says. Playing slowly and loudly reduces variables and simplifies the music, enabling you to focus almost entirely on maintaining good technique while your brain makes connections using both procedural and developmental memory.

Although you can Boot Camp any piece, Ms. Kondonassis often starts out her new recruits on a training regimen of Boot Camping single notes, scales, and simple exercises. Like pushups for the fingers, we gained strength as we were taught how to maintain perfect technique while plucking single, repeated notes slowly and loudly. As our technique improved, we were allowed to move on to Boot Camping real pieces of repertoire. The results were tremendous. Not only did our technique get better, but our fingers became stronger, our pieces were learned at a much faster rate, and our memory grew to be more reliable. All because of Boot Camp.

Basic training

The point of Boot Camp is to boil everything down to the basics. The two main elements of Boot Camp help a practicer to focus on the fundamentals. The first element of Boot Camp is to practice *slowly.* All you have to do is take the tempo down to an almost excruciating *Lento.* Practice in slow motion, being mindful about the notes and the patterns, making connections that will be helpful later. Since you are playing so slowly, you have time to pursue higher levels of perfection your technique—is there tension anywhere? Are your shoulders relaxed? Play through the passage this way a few times, making more connection each time you comb back through.

The second element of Boot Camp is to practice *at a single volume (loudly if possible).* Playing loudly will be helpful for many of you, such as harpists, pianists and string players. If you play an instrument that limits the amount of time you can safely play at a loud volume (e.g., brass and woodwinds), no worries: the main idea is to play at a single volume. Don't worry about the dynamics or articulations yet—play everything at a methodical monotone in order to focus on the notes.

Boot Camp Modifications for Instruments

Boot camp may have been formulated by a harpist, but with some slight modifications it can be a discipline used by most instrumentalists. There is no question about the benefits of the first element of boot camp for every musician: slow, methodical practice is recommended by experts of every instrument. As cellist Richard Weiss says, "The art of slow-motion practicing is critical to achieving virtuosity." But the second element, volume, might have slight variance depending on what instrument you play. Here are some breakdowns for Boot Camp for some different instrument categories that require modification, with quotes from the experts.

Brass: "The trombone pedagogue Per Brevig used to say to me, *slow practice equals fast progress*," says Brittany Lasch, trombone professor at Bowling Green State University. "Slow playing is excellent for muscle memory in both the arm (for trombone) or fingers (valved instruments) but also for the delicate muscles of the lips and the diaphragm and all other muscles involved in breathing." Instead of combining *slow* and *loud*, Lasch suggests that winds and brass players try the combination of *slow* and *soft*. "Soft practice is often overlooked," she says, adding that practicing softly is not only useful in order to save your chops, but it also helps you to prepare for exposed soft passages in brass orchestral repertoire. "If soft, delicate playing is not practiced regularly, it cannot be a reliable skill spontaneously."

Woodwinds: "To master a fast and challenging passage requires a great deal of patience," says concert flutist Beomjae Kim. "You eventually want the maximum efficiency of your finger movement, and also effortless breath control." His answer to mastering movement and breath control is to combine slow practice with overemphasizing finger motion on your instrument. First, play slowly. "As you are working on the passage slowly, pay attention to the notes you are playing. Remember the intervals, the pitches, and vocalize the passage in your head while executing it on your instrument slowly," Kim says.

> *"The art of slow-motion practicing is critical to achieving virtuosity."*
>
> — *Richard Weiss*

What he suggests next is to exaggerate your finger motion from one note to another. "This work at first feels very tedious, but the exaggeration enables your brain to memorize the finger movement." The result is a perfect combination of procedural and developmental memory (more on this in Chapter 18), resulting in a better grasp of the music. "The logic of this is that if you can hear the music in your head, then your muscles will follow."

Benefits of Boot Camp

Boot Camp is almost always helpful. Use it to warm up, and you will be well-oiled both physically and mentally for a productive practice session. Use it to isolate technique, and you will more swiftly be able to identify causes and cures. Use it on brand new notes, and you'll make connections and learn the music faster. Use it on a piece you're re-learning from years ago, and you will find that you recall the notes more quickly. Use it on any technically challenging or fast-paced passage, and you'll find that you are able to play it up to tempo with more accuracy.

"In my own practice, I use it almost every day in some fashion," Ms. Kondonassis says. Be sure that you don't over-stress or injure yourself by doing too much of it—Ms. Kondonassis suggests 15-20 minutes of boot camp per hour of practice as a healthy limit for productive practicing. "I find that it tends to speed up learning and make the whole practice session more solid and productive."

If you incorporate Boot Camp into your practice sessions, you may be surprised by how much calmer and more confident you feel. I can't tell you how many times I have come to a practice session in a frenzied, stressed state because of what I needed to accomplish, and calmed down

"If you incorporate Boot Camp into your practice sessions, you may be surprised by how much calmer and more confident you feel."

completely by spending just fifteen minutes in Boot Camp. Being able to isolate a difficult passage and play it confidently, strongly, and loudly at a tempo that is achievable makes me feel like I could conquer the world.

Yolanda Kondonassis' ingenious Boot Camp method is one of the most helpful practice techniques I have ever incorporated into my practice room philosophy. All of the harp students at CIM may have only committed to signing up for one semester of Boot Camp, but each of us in turn came to believe in it ourselves—and most of us continue to use this method long after graduation. Before your next practice session, sign up for Boot Camp. Incorporating Boot Camp into your practice sessions will equip you with everything needed to march to victory.

Review Questions

Question No. 1

What are the two elements of Boot Camp? Why do you think these are important in the practice room?

Question No. 2

What are the benefits of Boot Camp?

Question No. 3

How can you incorporate Boot Camp on your instrument?

≈ 13 ≈

Your Metronome
Is Your Best Friend

"The best way to learn
is through the powerful force of rhythm."

— W.A. Mozart

When I was a kid, my metronome's name was Fred Astaire.

It wasn't my idea. Growing up, the three of us kids shared a BOSS Dr. Beat. Our Dr. Beat was the best metronome model: it had all the levers and knobs, and it was capable of tapping subdivisions, meters, and complex cross rhythms. Despite all the fancy bells and whistles, though, none of us really *loved* to use our metronome. That is, until my little brother came home one day from his cello lesson.

"Mr. Weinstein told me that I need to become best friends with my metronome," Justin announced, "So I'm giving it a name."

We had been on a 1950's Musicals kick, so he decided on Fred Astaire (Why Fred Astaire, you ask? Well, have you ever seen anyone with more rhythmic precision?). Though naming a metronome might seem a little silly to you, it was a turning point for us little practicers. We started to really develop a relationship with our metronome in a much more tangible way. It was an essential part of every practice session. We came to trust it, listen to it, and use it as the standard for developing good rhythm. And eventually, as time progressed, each one of us came to actually love and look forward to our daily practice time with Fred Astaire.

> *"Get over any presumptions that metronomes are constricting, boring, or unnecessary. Those are all outright lies."*

Whether or not you actually name it, your metronome really should become your favorite practice companion. It should be an essential tool for developing good internal rhythm and for taking your skills to the next level. Get over any presumptions that metronomes are constricting, boring, or unnecessary. Those are all outright lies. I firmly believe that the metronome is one of the greatest inventions (right up there with the printing press and penicillin)! Here are a few secrets to using your metronome well.

Your metronome knows better than you. Metronomes really are the Boss! When your metronome is on, you *must* commit to its precision. Listen to your metronome carefully before you begin a passage to get into the right groove of the tempo. But don't stop there. Be sure to begin your passage exactly on the beat, and keep one ear absolutely focused on that click as you continue, requiring absolute precision of yourself. You may be tempted to relax your focus as the passage continues, but resist the urge. A metronome is of no use to you if you don't completely listen to it and learn how to be precise.

Your metronome is the fastest way to reach your tempo goals. You may think that it's not essential to use your metronome for getting your rep up to tempo. But in my experience, it's the only road to take. A favorite method for getting a difficult passage up to tempo is to take a microsection of the passage (a couple of bars, or even just a couple of beats) and put the metronome on a tempo at least twice as slow as you can play it. Use the #3xperfectly rule, repeating the microsection three times in a row perfectly before upping the tempo. Only go up three to six clicks at a time. Repeat this exercise until you're at your goal tempo for the day. Then move on to the next microsection! When you have two microsections up to tempo, don't forget to go back and play both sections together using the same #3xperfectly rule to fuse them into your memory.

You can cultivate internal rhythm with your metronome. A metronome shouldn't just keep you steady only while it's on. Learn how to internalize your rhythm by being selective about when you use it. Try playing a passage without a metronome first. Then, repeat the passage with the metronome on. Do you feel where you aren't precise with it? Are there any pulls to drag or rush? Isolate those sections with the metronome and then play the passage without the metronome again. Listen critically to notice where you have improved!

Another way to internalize rhythm is by practicing a Dalcroze Eurhythmics exercise: The Cosmic Whole Note. Put the metronome on a cosmically slow tempo (The standard is 6 beats per minute—you can achieve this on many modern metronomes and metronome apps by setting it to 36 BPM with six pulses, but taking out the sounds of all but the first pulse) and figure out how to clap exactly on the beat by walking subdivisions of the beat. Practice clapping on the beat four times in a row. After several practice sessions, challenge your internal rhythm by thinking the subdivisions rather than walking them. Over time, your internal rhythm may become so strong that you'll be able to clap on the beat without even thinking the subdivisions!

> *"Try playing a passage without a metronome first. Then, repeat the passage with the metronome on. Do you feel where you aren't precise with it?"*

Turn the metronome off for expressive practicing. The point at which the metronome isn't as helpful is when you're working on the expressive side of music, such as dynamics, rubato, phrasing etc. Be sure to turn the metronome off when you're experimenting with expression so that you will have the silence to listen to the changing moods and colors of the work and think with lines and phrases larger than the beat.

Your metronome has the potential to grow you, push you to the next level, develop your inner rhythm, and keep you honest as you seek to achieve your most ambitious practice goals. Use these techniques and you just might surprise yourself one day by saying, "My metronome really is my best friend!"

Review Questions

Question No. 1

Why is metronome use important? What are the benefits of using your metronome?

Question No. 2

When should you turn your metronome off?

Question No. 3

Reflect: What are some obstacles or ways that you could improve with rhythm? How could a metronome help you overcome these obstacles?

≋ 14 ≋

Be A
Stable-Mucker

"Don't judge each day by the harvest you reap
but by the seeds that you plant."

— *Robert Louis Stevenson*

There is intriguing wisdom in the biblical proverb: "Where there are no oxen, the manger is clean, but abundant crops come by the strength of the ox." In other words, taking care of oxen is hard and dirty work. Wouldn't you rather be in charge of a stable that never had to be mucked? You could sleep in, get to work at your leisure and take as much time off as you wanted. But the man with a dirty stable owns more value. The more oxen one has the more harvest one can bring in.

Achieving goals takes slow, laborious work of the stable mucking variety. To be a stable-mucker, you must endure grueling labor. It might seem like a boring and messy job, but a farmer knows that if he cares wholeheartedly for his property and his livestock, it will benefit him the most in the long run. He finds purpose in his stable mucking because of his property's value. Any good farmer is willing to become a stable-mucker when he understands his harvest is at stake.

Success requires not only hard work, but hard work combined with steadiness, strategy, and zero haste. I like to pair that proverb with a quote from the famous violin pedagogue Schiniki Suzuki who said, "Without stopping, without haste, carefully taking a step at a time forward will surely get you there." Slow, steady, wholehearted progress is the secret to meeting your goals.

Without haste

I'm blessed enough to live on a mountain in the beautiful Blue Ridge Mountain range in Virginia, with a trail that measures a 4-mile loop from my house to the overlook and back down. The interesting thing about the particular route I like to take is that the bulk of the incline happens in the first mile. It is steep and arduous, but once you achieve it, the remainder of the hike is easy. When I first started hiking the loop, my impatience to get to the top propelled me to take on that first mile at much too fast a pace. Speed was my only interest. I booked it to the top as fast as I could, feeling accomplished by my endurance and tenacity. Once I finished that first mile, though, a wave of dizziness overcame me and my head started pounding. I had worked hard and accomplished the most difficult part of the journey, but the pace at which I moved kept me from enjoying the view—not only the overlook at the top, but all the beautiful scenes along the way.

Like pacing myself around my 4-mile loop, I have also learned to pace myself in my journey with the harp. If you have a competitive or passionate spirit like me, you can probably identify with the urge I tend to have to meet my biggest goals as quickly as possible. But I hope you'll learn that life is a lot like hiking a mountain. If you burn yourself out, you'll have spent your whole life working toward the future and when that future comes, you won't have anything left in you to enjoy it.

Without stopping

Achieving success is only possible for those who are willing to work on a slow incline towards the top. But they also must work steadily. It reminds me of taking music lessons as a young student. "Don't rush," my teacher would often tell me. If one rushes the music, the listener is left feeling uneasy. Even if they can't articulate that you are rushing, they will know something is wrong. But just as often, she would say, "Don't drag." You can just as easily swing the pendulum the other way. If you drag the tempo in a piece, your listener will feel stuck, as though your piece will never end. I quickly learned as a young music student that I needed to

"Achieving success is only possible for those who are willing to work on a slow incline towards the top."

dedicate some quality time with my good friend Fred Astaire in order to learn how to neither drag nor rush. I wanted to be a great musician, and great musicians play steadily.

Great musicians live steadily, too. When strategizing how to accomplish their goals, they learn that it won't work to rush to the top. But they also learn that nothing is ever achieved by dawdling by the side of the trail. When it comes to practicing, we tend to look for the shortcut, the hack, the secret. We cut corners and tell ourselves that the easier road is the better road. We want to be the best at our instrument—but we want it *now.* Most of the time we don't really feel like doing whatever it takes to achieve it.

But it doesn't work that way. Those who succeed tell themselves that the end goal is worth it. They know what the view is like at the top, and that desire to see it propels them forward. They don't hurry, but they don't stop either. Willingly and joyfully, they put their backs into their work because the end goal gives them purpose and drive.

Mucking is messy

The stable-mucking proverb teaches us that hard work has value. But it also teaches us that hard work can be messy. It's slow and steady labor, but it can also be unpleasant at times. A good farmer knows that in light of the harvest, the mess is worth it. In your practice room, be willing to get messy in order to achieve. What steps can you take in your practice session today that gets you closer to learning that piece, fixing that technique problem, winning that audition? How can you be a stable-mucker, working steadily, willfully, joyfully toward your goal?

Next time you're in the middle of a grueling practice session, with little progress and so many problems to fix, remind yourself of this proverb. Being a musician requires patience, hard work, lots of maintenance, and thousands of hours of stable-mucking. Without all that hard work you wouldn't be where you are, and without continuing in that hard work you won't be able to achieve the results to come. Don't slack. Do the dirty work. Be a stable-mucker, and work hard in order to bring an abundant harvest home.

Review Questions

Question No. 1

According to this chapter, what is the secret to meeting your goals?

Question No. 2

How is your musical journey like hiking a mountain?

Question No. 3

Why is it important to methodically pursue your goals through relentless, hard work?

≈ 15 ≈

Don't Be A Trained Bird

"Don't give notes—give the meaning of the notes!"

— *Pablo Casals*

I've always loved songbirds more than pet parrots. Don't get me wrong though—I think parrots are brilliant creatures! Did you know that an African Grey Parrot is able to speak a vocabulary of up to a thousand words? As amazing as that is to me, I have always felt that there was something rather mechanical about a parrot's voice. Though a pet parrot might be smart, they are only replicating sounds their trainers teach them. There is nothing intentional about what the parrot says, because he has just been trained to mimic someone else. But a songbird has its own melody.

I wish I could take you for a walk around my mountain neighborhood. We have songbirds galore: finches, nuthatches, woodpeckers, bluebirds, towhees, cardinals, sparrows, warblers, titmice, thrushes, chickadees.

Each one has a unique song, and each song is uniquely beautiful. There is a certain depth about a songbird's melody—its musicality, its innocence, its boldness, its joy, its freedom. And as I walk through the forests in the mountains, each unique song rises up to meet another in a cacophony of beautiful sound.

I hear a lot in a simple songbird's melody that makes me love them more than parrots. He has been given a song to sing, and not a day goes by that he fails to wake up in the morning and belt it out, loud and clear. It is *his* song, and his purpose in life is to boldly and unashamedly sing his heart out. That's probably why Carl Philip Emmanuel Bach, the son of Johann Sebastian, once said, "You have to make music from the soul, not like a trained bird." Don't be a trained bird who heartlessly imitates others. Be more like a songbird. Belt out your song from the heart, and let your own unique voice ring out.

Playing expressively

Playing from the heart is not as easy as one might think. Like most things in life, expression must be practiced to be mastered. Playing expressively is not something a great musician improvises in a performance. Every phrase is carefully thought out beforehand, scrutinized, strategized, and memorized. And as in most other disciplines, learning how to be more instinctive in your musical expression is a gradual process that is mastered with practice. Playing expressively goes far beyond the notes on the page or even the dynamics and expressive markings written. Like a songbird, you have a certain depth about you—you must reach deeper to find that depth. Go beyond the notes on the page and read between the lines. You have so much you can say with your music. How will you say it?

Interpreting music well

When seeking to learn how to interpret music well, it is best to start with the basics and a thorough study of the piece. Once the notes of your piece are learned and up to tempo, pay close attention to articulations, tempo changes, dynamic changes, and Italian expressive markings. Take your phone off Airplane Mode and pull up Google Translate if you don't understand what terms mean, or invest in a music dictionary. Get a grasp of exactly how the composer wanted you to express their music. Before you add any of your own phrasing and expression, you should be true to the composer's wishes for the piece.

Secondly, become informed about the history of the piece. Understand the era, culture, and genre in which it was written. Look at other art from that time frame: paintings, decorative arts, landscapes, dance. Listen to other music of that era from different composers. Find out more about the composer and why they might have written the piece. Was it written in dedication to anyone? Does it reflect the composer's personal life? Is the piece based on a poem or otherwise programmatic? If so, what is the story? The more you know, the more informed your interpretation of the piece will be.

Next, look at the piece as a whole. What are the piece's main sections? Get out a pencil and number them. What is the form of the piece? Does the piece have a climax or multiple climaxes? If so, how does this inform your expressive decisions? Give some thought to these things. You should also decide on the moods and emotions of the piece. What would you say about the overall mood? Are there contrasting sections with different emotions? Mark all of the things you notice in your music (or if you want to keep your music clean, use sticky notes).

After you have looked at the piece as a whole, start looking at the smaller sections. Don't just play the music beat by beat, measure by measure. Look at the phrases and mark them. Are they 4-bar or 8-bar phrases, or are they asymmetrical? What are these phrases saying? Consider giving descriptive words to each phrase. Be creative, don't just write "happy" or "sad." Consider these adjectives: *pensive, agitated, reflective, hopeful, restless, ecstatic, melancholy, frenzied, incensed, peaceful, despondent, victorious, innocent, bubbly, skeptical, lovesick, nostalgic, free.*

In those phrases, consider the voicing. Are you playing just a melody line, or are there other voices underneath (a secondary melody and bass line)? Study the contour of these lines. How do they blend together and interact with each other? Is there a conversation going on between them? Where are they leading? What is the climax of the phrase and how do you lead the listener's ear there? Remember, an average listener's ear won't be able to take in everything you play in one hearing.

Your job is to show your audience what to listen for in the piece. You are guiding their ears. Highlight the most important thing you want a listener to take away from each phrase, and consider how you can lead them there.

Next, look at the chord structure. If your piece has accompaniment, study the score and listen to a recording. Which chords are the most special or "juicy?" Are there dissonances that resolve that you can bring out? Are there sequences or recurring chord patterns? What can you do to bring attention to these important chords and to make those moments more memorable? For me, I can make chords special on the harp by creating a different attack, squeezing the strings differently, raising faster or slower, rolling the chord a different way, playing lower in the strings to get a different color, adding an accent or subito piano, and a hundred other ways. There are countless colors you can get on your instrument to make moments special. Experiment with this.

Once you have decided how you want to phrase each section of your piece, consider the transitions. How are you going to transition from a "pensive" section to a "victorious" section? What expressive markings are already there to help you? Consider how you can use volume, speed, and silence to aid in making the transition smooth.

Every note plays a role in the story

Once you have thoroughly studied the piece, think less objectively about it. Ultimately, you want to tell a story with the piece. It doesn't have to be a story with a plot (a castle, a love triangle, a duel, and a happily ever after), although it can be. But once you have a good grasp of the objective details of the piece, you should start asking yourself what the main idea is and what you most want to communicate with it. Is it about courage in the face of adversity? Is it about the simplicity of home? Is it about love triumphing over sorrow? Decide what your story is and let that inform your expressive decisions.

Once you decide on your story, treat every note like a role in a play. Some may seem less important than others, but they all have unique roles which make them indispensable. Good musicians follow all dynamics and expressive markings, but a true artist gives weight to every note. She makes thoughtful decisions about how each one fits into the story. If a note is not a major character in the story, then it is leading us to one that is.

Don't be afraid to explore

The only way to master the art of interpretation is to get in the practice room and get messy. Don't be afraid to spend lots of time experimenting with different ideas, even the seemingly wild ones! As a general rule, I always tell my students to "overdo" expression in the practice room. Having too much starting out is OK because you can always rein it in. Experiment with how many colors you can add to your palate. Work toward getting as many emotions out of your instrument as you can. Remember, a practice haven is a really safe place to try new things.

As you can see, interpreting a piece is a multilayered process with hundreds of expressive decisions. Once you make those hundreds of decisions and settle on how you want to interpret your piece, own it. Put in the work and the time to decide exactly how you want to express the music, but once you have decided, own it as your personal and unique work of art. Believe in every single note and play courageously. As a songbird bravely belts out his melody in a deep forest, so you should own your piece and communicate it to your audience unashamedly. Don't play like a trained bird. Let every note sing.

Review Questions

Question No. 1

Like a songbird, you have a certain depth about you. How can you use music in order to communicate that depth to others?

Question No. 2

Interpretation requires careful study of your piece of repertoire. What are some ways you can study your piece in order to understand and interpret it better?

Question No. 3

Pick one of the pieces you are working on. What story do you want to tell with it? How can you use every note of your piece to communicate that story to your audience?

≈16≈

Record Yourself

"I listened more than I studied, therefore little by little my knowledge and ability were developed."

— *Joseph Haydn*

My decision to become an active Instagram user proved to be life-changing in a way that I never expected: the motivating lifestyle of recording myself on a daily basis propelled me forward in almost every way. My technique improved immensely, my lyrical passages sung more, my ear became fine-tuned, and my rhythm and pacing improved. It helped me grow personally as well. I became more confident in my playing and performing for others, I developed a level of authenticity and connection as I banded together with my Instagram community, and eventually I came to expect bigger and better things from myself. Self-recording is an undervalued but highly effective way to improve in the practice room. Learn how to hear yourself as an audience member rather than a performer, and you will be surprised by how much you grow.

For the record

Why is self-recording so effective in a practice session? Alan Bise, the Grammy Award-winning recording engineer and producer of Azica Records, weighs in. "The only stimuli an audio recording provides is sound," he says. "There is no visual, no scent, nothing." By recording yourself in a practice room and listening back through the recording, you can focus your attention more thoroughly on the music, thereby fine-tuning your ears to listen more precisely.

Bise also says that recording yourself is a great way to gain better focus in a practice session and learn how to perform with more accuracy. "You can't fake it in a recording, or it will be heard," Bise says. "I tell my first time recording clients to look at the most difficult passages of their music. By session time, you should reliably be able to nail them at tempo (and I mean nailed, not faked pretty well!) three out of five times. If you can hit

"By recording yourself in a practice room and listening back through the recording, you can focus your attention more thoroughly on the music, thereby fine-tuning your ears to listen more precisely."

three out of five, you can probably get one out of five in the session."

Self-recording is also an effective way to simulate a performance and study the way you might react under duration of stress. "From a performance standpoint, recording is the only type of playing you will do where the tension can rise over time, as opposed to release." Bise says. In his career as an audio engineer, Bise has noticed that even if a musician can play a passage perfectly in a practice session, they may not be able to play it as perfectly when performing or recording. Even if they can confidently play in practice, they choke under pressure. Bise recalls one day in which he performed an experiment that proved this to be true:

"An artist was having a difficult time with a passage that was normally not a problem. Many takes later, the frustration level was high. Since I didn't see any improvement on the horizon, I said I needed to excuse myself to the men's room and asked him to practice the passage for a few minutes. I left the talkback mic on and stood, opened the squeaky door, closed it, and sat right back down and put on headphones. Of course, as he casually practiced he nailed it two or three times. I did the reverse trick with the doors and, in his mind, I was back from the men's room ready to do more takes. He did the next take, and it was ok, but not as good as his practice. Of course, I used the practice material and never told him in case I needed to use that trick again!"

You may be surprised when you press the record button by how much your heart-rate rises. This is nothing to worry about—it just proves how helpful recording yourself will be as you seek to become a performer unperturbed by nerves. If you consistently record yourself you'll notice improvements in stress or anxiety. Overcoming self-recording anxiety will ultimately help you learn how to overcome performance anxiety.

Self-recording can be a great way to improve your game in the practice room. But you might ask, "Is it ever unhelpful to record yourself?" Bise offers his thoughts. "I think anytime you can hear yourself, it can be helpful," he says. "Keep in mind that microphones CAN lie about frequency response and tone color. But they don't lie about noises, rhythm, missed notes and the all important vibe." Especially noises, Bise says. Often musicians will come into his studio not even realizing that there is extraneous, unwanted noise in their playing that could easily be eliminated with practice.

Equipment

If recording yourself is so helpful when practicing, you may wonder if you should invest in fancy equipment in order to hear yourself better. Jared Hall, my older brother, is a professional photographer and filmmaker (and the brains behind all of my music videos). He always insists that it's most important to use what you are comfortable with. "Even though there's a real difference in using a Stradivarius violin, it's the performer that makes the magic happen. How you use your equipment is much more important than the equipment that you use." Even using the Voice Memo app on your phone can be a helpful way to self-record in a practice session. That being said, there are a few pieces of equipment that will be valuable if you are serious about improving yourself through self-recording.

Headphones. "A normal pair of earbuds will work in a pinch," Jared says, but he recommends the Sennheiser HD280PRO for a quality pair of headphones.

Microphone. Don't go overboard—it's always a good idea to start small, especially if you're planning to primarily use your microphone for practice sessions and social media posts. For my personal practice time and my Instagram recordings, I use a Rode VideoMicro. This little microphone connects straight to my iPhone with an adaptor cable (a 3.5mm TRS to TRRS microphone cable adaptor). This makes recording for Instagram posts extremely easy and improves the sound quality! Another device that my brother and I recommend is the Zoom H4N Pro. As an all-in-one recording device,

"Microphones can lie about frequency response and tone color. But they don't lie about noises, rhythm, missed notes and the all important vibe."

it's a great starting point that also accepts more expensive external microphones if you decide to upgrade later on. Bise highly recommends mics in the Audio Technica series, such as the AT-8024. These are relatively affordable options for the quality.

Recording Software. Garage Band is a great place to start if you're a Mac user. If you own a Windows or Linux, you could use Audacity, another free program that is downloadable online. Although there are many more expensive options to explore, a program that is accessible and comfortable is more valuable to you.

Video camera. "If you have a little budget, the Sony ADR-FX33 makes a very nice video for the price," Bise says, but he adds that using your phone will also work just fine. I agree: I usually use my trusty iPhone for Instagram videos and personal practicing. It's handy and does a decent job for daily practice posts.

No matter how much equipment you decide to invest in, the most important thing to remember is what you are able to get out of the recording process. As Jared says, "It's not about the equipment you use, it's about the story you tell."

Recording in practice

What are the best steps we can take to use self-recording to improve ourselves? Here are some practical ways to get the most out of self-recording in your practice room. You can record yourself in order to:

Listen to your dynamics and phrasing. Are you making them as contrasted as you think? Consider looking at the audio waves on Garage Band for a visual representation of your phrases. Remember, this may not be a completely accurate representation of what the audience will hear, but it can give you a good idea, and visualizing the sound can help.

Check your notes and rhythm. Listen carefully: Do you ever rush or drag? Is your rhythm right? Any wrong notes? Read the music while you listen to yourself. Where are the inconsistencies?

Inspect your technique. Are there extraneous noises you wouldn't otherwise notice? Is your breathing noticeable? Is there buzzing anywhere? Is your technique messy at all? What steps can you take to make your performance cleaner?

Watch your form from a video. Are you slouching? Are you maintaining good technique? How is your hand position? Any tension? Are you raising your shoulders? Think about how your technique can improve just from looking at yourself in the video. If you were the teacher, what would you say to yourself?

Conduct with the music. Are you working on a part that fits into an ensemble or orchestra? Yolanda Kondonassis suggests recording yourself in preparation for fitting into that texture: "Whenever I have a part that needs to fit into the intricate puzzle of an ensemble work, I will often record or videotape myself and then conduct the tape to make sure I'm in the rhythmic 'pocket.' It's a great way to test yourself when every split second is important."

Simulate a performance and practice for an upcoming concert or recital. This is not only a helpful way to put yourself into "performance mode" for recital run-through, but it's also a great method for practicing because you can listen back for any imperfections and work toward making your piece that much more polished (More on this in Chapter 19).

Compare your recording to your favorite artist performing the same piece. What are the differences in your playing? What needs to be done in the practice room in order to get to that next level of playing?

Post your progress to social media platforms like Instagram. If you make a promise to post a practice video every day, you are more likely to do whatever it takes to make that clip sound good enough to post. But posting your practice videos is also a great way to become more vulnerable, accept suggestions from friends, and share your work in a place outside of yourself and your practice room.

The hashtag #PurposeInPractice is a community of musicians committed to growing together.

The hashtag #PurposeInPractice is a community designed for this very purpose, so consider banding with the team of musicians committed to growing through recording, sharing, and learning together.

I cannot express enough how important self-recording is to the development of a practicing musician. It is absolutely vital to your growth and improvement to hear yourself as others hear you, to be the most helpful critic for yourself, and to pursue higher versions of perfection. My newfound process of recording and listening to myself consistently has shaped me in ways I never imagined—and if you record yourself, it will shape you, too.

Review Questions

Question No. 1

Why is recording yourself in the practice room important? Name three reasons.

Question No. 2

The most important thing about equipment is that you use what is accessible and comfortable. What equipment do you have that would enable you to start self-recording in your practice room today?

Question No. 3

What are two or three techniques you can try today that incorporate recording yourself?

≈ 17 ≾

Become A Student
of the Greatest Artists

"People err who think my art comes easily to me. I assure you, dear
friend, nobody has devoted so much time and thought to compo-
sitions as I. There is not a famous master whose music I have not
industriously studied through many times."

— W.A. Mozart

I magine this for a moment: It's a typical Monday
evening, and you are practicing in your practice
room as usual. Suddenly, to your surprise, Yo Yo
Ma casually walks in.

"I just wanted to give you some tips on your piece,"
he says. He sits down and plays it for you, explaining
the way he phrases the passages. You pinch yourself.
Am I dreaming?

He stands up with his cello and heads to the door as
you thank him profusely for his time. But Yo-Yo Ma isn't
gone for more than five seconds before you hear a rap at
the door again. It's Hilary Hahn.

"I was in the area and I thought I'd stop in," she
says. "Your playing is great, but I have a secret for this
passage that I'd love for you to try."

Can this really be happening? You hang on to every word she says.

"Gotta run to catch my plane," she announces, and before you know it, she's gone too.

Yo-Yo Ma and Hilary Hahn in one day? It's unbelievable. But your mind is blown further when your practice room door opens again!

"Just stopping by," Lang Lang says. *Are you kidding me?!* "I heard you practicing a piece I know by heart. Why don't we play it together?"

It's the best day of your life, although by this point you're seriously worried about your sanity. Three of the world's most loved classical musicians offering you their best advice in your personal practice room, all in one day? You have got to be the luckiest person on the planet.

You can invite the greatest artists into your practice room

What if three of today's greatest artists volunteered to come into your studio and help you grow? How valuable would that be? What do you think that would be worth? As unbelievable as that scenario sounds, you might be surprised for me to tell you that you have something even more valuable at your fingertips. You can have access to not just three, but *virtually all* of the world's greatest artists. You can invite each one into your practice room, becoming a student of the greatest artists.

One of the best things for musicians that came out of the twentieth century was the recording industry. Just the possibilities, the avenues this opened up, were amazing. Artists could perform their best version of a work with a microphone and then send it out to reach a much larger audience. As they did so, their most perfected performance was preserved as a legacy to each new generation. It's indisputable that the recording industry raised the bar for performers: having an opportunity to make a lasting imprint in an iconic recording made them strive harder to reach the next level of perfection and artistry.

Take a quick look at your phone. With this device, you have the power to summon virtually all the world's greatest artists to your practice room for wisdom and direction. At your fingertips, you have access to the highest-caliber performances of the world's finest musicians. Why wouldn't you take the time to benefit from being a student of the greatest artists?

> *"You have the power to summon virtually all the world's greatest artists to your practice room for wisdom and direction."*

Recording study, step-by-step

For every piece you are currently learning, you should be spending a good chunk of time listening to recordings of that work. First, do some quick research to see which artists have recorded the piece in question. It's great to get perspective on your pieces from non-professionals, but primarily listen to recordings from well-respected recording artists. Once you have a list of recordings you want to study, choose the one that looks the best. Take out your best headphones, pull it up on iTunes or Spotify, and get ready for an intense practice session of listening.

Your first time listening to the recording should be all the way through, start to finish. Get a sense of the overarching story and feel of the piece. First of all, what do you like about this performance? Study their technique, their expression, their performance art. Ask yourself, what makes them great? What is the most valuable thing that I can learn from them?

Your second listen should be a little more in depth. Get out your music and some little sticky notes and read along while you listen. This time, consider phrasing and subtlety. Pause the recording when you get to something you really like and want to emulate, or even things you don't particularly like and want to avoid. If a passage struck you as particularly clean or excellent or poignant, mark it. These are all sections for later study.

Next is the gleaning stage. Go back to those sections you marked and study each one intensely. Listen to the isolated passage and ask yourself some questions. What did they have to do technically in order to make this emotion come across? Are they using accents or stressing specific notes? How are they using rubato to tell their story? How are they using silence to add drama? How do they transition between sections? Be specific and use your ear critically. Glean all you can and then move on to the next small section.

Finally, once you have your piece up to tempo you should try playing along with the recording. This has proven to be extremely beneficial for me because it forces me to match their exact pacing. It's like having the superpower of morphing yourself into that artist for a few minutes! This method to study can help you mature immensely as you seek to become a more expressive musician.

Once you have gone through this listening process, wash, rinse, repeat. Take a mental break, but then be sure to go back and repeat with a different recording artist. Never listen to only one recording of your piece. This limits your growth and learning. You have thousands of recording artists at your fingertips, so use that privilege to give yourself as much to work with as you can!

Inform your ears

While listening to multiple recordings of your piece is important, you should also spend some time listening to other pieces in the genre or by the same composer. Learning a Bach suite? Don't limit yourself to the one you are working on—Bach has dozens of suites for you to comb through to get a feel for the pacing of dance movements. Are you playing a piece by Debussy? It would be tragic to only listen to your piece when you could gain a more complete sense of his style through his other works. But don't stop there! Extend your listening experience to other composers of the Impressionist movement, as well as composers belonging to other eras and genres influential to Debussy. Anything like this that you can pour through your ears will be helpful to sift through as you work toward perfecting your piece and making it a true work of art.

> *"You have thousands of recording artists at your fingertips, so use that privilege to give yourself as much to work with as you can!"*

Is your piece a transcription? If so, there are a few things to keep in mind. First of all, be sure you listen to the piece in its original form. For example, if I as a harpist am learning Debussy's First Arabesque, I should primarily listen to a variety of pianists performing the piece since the work was originally written for piano. But I should also listen to multiple recordings of harpists, as well as other instrumentalists, to gain different perspectives. Sometimes, the same piece on a different instrument sounds totally different. Phrasings which would be idiomatic to one instrument might translate as unnatural to a different instrument. It is helpful and extremely eye-opening to study this.

Outside from the music on your stand, you should be listening to artists from a variety of instruments and genres. If you are a guitarist, you should not just be listening to guitar music. Listen to all instruments. If you are working on solo music, try listening not just to soloists but different chamber combinations and orchestras. If you are a classical musician, expand your listening experience to jazz, folk music, funk, rock, etc. The more you listen, the more informed your ear becomes, and the more tools you add to your toolbox as you seek to add nuance and artistry to your music.

The potential you have to learn from the recordings of all the greatest artists is even more valuable than if your favorite three musicians spent an hour with you in a practice room. For one thing, you have a vast, inexhaustible treasure trove of recordings to study. For another thing, these are the most perfected versions of each artist. They sound better in these recordings than they ever have, and you have the opportunity to dissect those recordings and figure out why they are so great. Investing your time in listening to great music is more valuable than your biggest imagination. Treat it that way. Listen to great recordings. Become a student of the greatest artists.

Review Questions

Question No. 1

Who do you deem the greatest artists in the world?

Question No. 2

Why is it important to regularly listen to their music?

Question No. 3

What are some ways that studying recordings of your current repertoire can help you learn and grow as a musician?

≋18≋

Memorize Methodically

"Energy and persistence conquer all things."

— *Benjamin Franklin*

I can vividly remember the worst performance I ever gave. It was back when I was a student at CIM. I presented a recital in a retirement home auditorium in Cleveland, which I had set up as a practice run for an upcoming competition. The room was packed full of elderly residents, most of whom were very well educated in classical music. Some of them were retired members of the Cleveland Orchestra, and one was even an accomplished harpist! I admit I felt a little intimidated, but I didn't feel fazed because my practice run-through that morning went smooth as butter. Everything worked, and I didn't have any memory slips. All my pedals moved to the right places at the right times and my hands knew exactly where to go. It was memorized, and I was ready.

Except I wasn't ready!

I walked to the stage to perform the recital, and it completely crashed and burned. There are always sections (I'm sure you can relate) that feel a little less confident than the others, which you might expect to crumble under pressure. But it wasn't just those spots—even the sections I felt the most confident about were a complete failure! Every piece was a train wreck. My only comfort was that even though I struggled to get through each piece, I managed to keep going and bravely plough through to the bitter end.

I was in a bit of a daze as I walked off stage. I had been so sure that it would be a grand slam performance. What had happened?

The danger of muscle memory

I used to always pride myself on my good muscle memory. It can be a huge advantage to be able to automatically memorize a piece from repetitive practice. Muscle memory is a great first step—even a necessary first step—toward total memorization. But I have learned the hard way that we should never entirely rely on it, because in cases of stress or performance anxiety, muscle memory is not always a reliable friend.

In neuro-speak, muscle memory falls into the "procedural memory" category. Procedural memory happens when you repeat a task over and over again until it becomes ingrained into your brain. You are able to remember it because your neurons connect those paths as you are doing the task, and afterward you find that you have achieved mastery over that task without recalling the exact moment when that memory became solidified.

Procedural memory is necessary for everyday life, and extremely helpful in the practice room. It can be helpful because it is a type of long-term memory. Think about your route to work or the way you instinctively catch a ball thrown at you. Many of the everyday skills you have in your long-term memory bank are because of your procedural memory. In a performance, this can be a huge advantage. Many times I have almost frozen as I anticipated upcoming passages in performances. "I can't remember what chords those are," I will think, or maybe I'll wonder, "What was that fingering, again?" In these moments I tell myself that, although I can't quite remember in the moment, I can trust that my muscles know where to go. Most of the time, they do and I perform those passages without a hitch!

The problem with procedural memory is that this doesn't always happen. For reasons scientists don't completely understand, under duration of stress and performance anxiety the brain can sometimes momentarily forget those actions and enter into a phase commonly referred to as "choking under pres-

> *"Procedural memory happens when you repeat a task over and over again until it becomes ingrained into your brain."*

sure." Because the brain only has procedural memory of the task, when we find ourselves under pressure that memory can temporarily go out the window and we are left floundering. That's exactly what happened in my recital.

Declarative memory

Thankfully for us, there is a different type of memory that neuroscientists call "declarative memory." If muscle memory is by rote, by learning *how* something is done, then declarative memory is by reason, by learning *why* something is done. It is a cognitive, logical study of the ins and outs of the task at hand. When you combine both procedural and declarative memory, you have a better chance of memorizing your music as your brain makes more connections to pull from. Basically, the more deeply you understand a piece the more completely you will be able to memorize the piece. There are many ways we can use declarative memory to our advantage. Here are the ones that have proven to be the most helpful for me.

"If muscle memory is by rote, by learning how something is done, then declarative memory is by reason, by learning why something is done."

Seeing. Get better at taking mental snapshots

of your music. Can you visualize it while you play it memorized? Writing your markings in bright colors (my favorite is red) can help a lot with this. Also look at the relationship between the music and your hands. Draw connections to the way intervals look on the music and on your instrument. Look for patterns in the music.

Hearing. A good understanding of music theory can help you with memorization. Analyze the chord progressions and melodic lines. Do you hear patterns in the music? If you are listening carefully while memorizing, your ear will make logical decisions that will translate to your playing.

Touching. Kinetic memory is very effective. How does the passage feel in your hands? Memorize the sensation of a certain fingering. Memorize how it feels to play every interval at your instrument. But also don't be afraid to get away from your instrument and feel the piece in other ways. Clap the rhythms, or step them. If you can feel the music in your hands or feet, you're more likely to translate them to your instrument more accurately.

Vocalizing. I'm a fan of talking to oneself while practicing, especially while memorizing! When working on memory, the discoveries I make are engrained even better if I say them out loud. Declaring what is there ("the melody goes down a half step here," or "this is a pattern of thirds that continues to this measure") helps to identify things quickly and add them to my memory bank.

Writing. Once you find things that work, write them down. It's a great idea to locate patterns in your music and write them in. Consider using colors in your music to highlight different parts you want to group together in your memory, or write down the different ways you memorized your piece in your practice journal.

Tips for memorization practice

As you seek to develop your procedural and declarative memory, here are some practical tips that will help:

Isolate microsections. Procedural and declarative memory are both most effective when working with small sections. If you want to memorize a piece, start with a tiny, isolated microsection, like a measure or even half a measure. You will learn the music by procedural memory with repetition, and you will further memorize with declarative memory when you take the time to study the microsection, locate patterns, and use the techniques above to understand the music more fully. Next, memorize the next microsection and don't forget to go back and fuse the sections together in your memory. It's sort of like piecing a quilt: you start with tiny remnants of

> *"If you want to memorize a piece, start with a tiny, isolated section, like a measure or even half a measure. I like to call these 'microsections.'"*

fabric and sew them together, one by one, until you have a full work of art.

Sing it. Sing the melody and think about how it feels in your voice. Notice the scales and leaps in the melody, and how much your voice has to jump up to reach a pitch. Feel the spacial difference of those intervals.

Test your memory away from your instrument. Step away from your instrument and see if you can think through and visualize the section you are memorizing without looking at the music. If you are unable to visualize it, chances are you are still relying on your muscle memory.

Try writing down the phrase. Get out some staff paper and see if you can write down the phrase you memorized. This will prove that you know it in your head, not just by heart.

Continue to test your memory by giving yourself performance opportunities. No matter how much we memorize, we don't ever *truly* know if our memory is fixed until we perform. If you are memorizing your piece for a big performance, set up smaller performances designed to test your memory. Try to recreate that feeling of pressure so that you can identify the weaker memory sections in the piece. That way you can go back to the practice room and adequately isolate them before the big day.

Muscle memory can be a huge advantage to your big performance, but it is risky to rely on it. Develop your declarative memory so that when you find yourself in a situation where you are under pressure, you don't have to choke. As uncomfortable as it was, my worst recital proved to be a great gift because it prodded me to develop a more reliable way to memorize. I hope that this in turn helps you as you build up a more reliable memory. A well-developed memorization method will give you peace and confidence on performance day.

Review Questions

Question No. 1

Take a moment to reflect on the best and worst performances you have given. Do you rely too much on your muscle memory to get you through a performance?

Question No. 2

In what ways is procedural (muscle) memory a helpful and necessary tool for performers? Why shouldn't we completely rely on it?

Question No. 3

What are some practical ways for you to be more methodical in your practice sessions by developing declarative memory?

Question No. 4

How can you use your senses to more fully comprehend the music you are learning?

≈ 19 ≈

Polish Toward
Perfection

"Every difficulty slurred over
will be a ghost to disturb your repose later on."

— *Frederic Chopin*

How do you switch from learning notes to making a piece performance-ready? Learning takes time—a lot of slow, methodical, efficient practice. A typical practice session should be goal oriented and focused on small victories: microsection isolation, good technique and rhythm, evenness of tone, and regular, slow, steady progress. But once you start getting close to your performance day, practice sessions should start to look a little different. You should move toward a mode of focus that takes your performance repertoire to the next level—polishing it in a way that pushes you toward a higher version of perfection.

Benefits of daily run-throughs

One to two weeks out from the performance, commit to doing a run-through of your performance repertoire every day. This might seem overwhelming, but I promise that it will prove to be extremely helpful for you as you prepare. Here are some tips for your daily run-through:

If you are performing more than one piece, decide on your performance order and play it that way every practice run-through. Give thought to the pieces that are most physically taxing: would it be easier for you to get those out of the way early in the program, or wait until you have warmed up with an easier work? Giving thought to these things as you practice a performance as a whole is important to get a perspective of the kind of energy it takes to move swiftly from one piece to the next.

When you do your daily run-through, make it seem as much like the performance as you can. Make sure you actually do run through the program: no stops, no backtracking to fix mistakes. As my first harp teacher Anastasia Jellison used to tell me, play "Loud and Proud," even through your worst memory slips.

As much as possible, try to perform your daily run-throughs at the same time your performance will be. This will condition your body to be ready to expend all of that energy on performance day.

Record your daily run-throughs. This is the very best pre-performance practice technique I have ever discovered, and will prove to be helpful to you in so many ways! First of all, recording locks you into a type of performance mode, where you are in a sense being "watched" by the camera. You will be more likely to stay honest and do true run-throughs, plowing through your program no matter what happens. Take this opportunity to practice turning off your "worst critic." Practice enjoying the performance and giving it your all. When you have finished your run-through, save the recording on your phone and get it out the next day at the beginning of your practice session. This is when you turn your "worst critic" back on. Listen through everything with a critical ear. Get out some small sticky notes and use them to mark mistakes, memory slips, and anything you'd like to do differently. Now, you have a practice plan for the day! Go through your recital rep, isolating the sections with the sticky notes. Take them off when you feel satisfied with them. Then do another run-through and start the process all over again. It's a refining process that forces you to have even higher standards for yourself every day, while also helping you become more comfortable playing through your whole program. By the time you get to the performance, it will be a piece of cake!

Mental preparation

One of the biggest things to master in the art of performing is the mind game. It is often said that when you get on stage, you should try to make it seem as much like "home" as you can. But sometimes this just isn't doable—it's hard to have that frame of mind when so much else is going on in your brain in the middle of a performance. It can be difficult to make the stage seem like your practice room. But you *can* take the time beforehand to make your practice room seem like a stage. Here are some practical ways to prepare mentally for your performance:

Put yourself through mildly "stressful" situations that might mimic a performance. Turn out all the lights except for a stand light to mimic a dark auditorium. Run up and down the stairs several times to get your heart pumping. Try doing a run-through without warming up. Do a run-through in front of someone who intimidates you. Get a friend to do distracting things to practice maintaining focus. Try to anticipate anything that could "go wrong" or throw you off in a performance setting, and figure out how you can focus such that nothing will faze you.

Make sure you play every note of your performance in your performance dress. This is a must! We tend to forget that what we wear changes the feel of our movement and even our instrument. Wear your performance dress to a practice session and ask yourself some questions: is it restricting in any way? Do you feel comfortable? Do you have to make any technical adjustments because of what you are wearing? Be sure you wear the complete dress: clothing, shoes, jewelry and accessories, and makeup (remember, a little lipstick goes a long way). Anticipate the way you will look and feel on performance day.

See if you can practice in the performance venue beforehand. It helps me so much as I prepare for a performance to be able to visualize the venue in my mind. It is also helpful because you can take time to get to know the acoustics and adjust your playing accordingly. If you get to practice at your venue beforehand, take time to mentally get a scope of the room and make a haven of it. "Own" it as your place to shine.

Visualize your victory

A helpful mind strategy is visualization. Visualization is a clinical technique that many athletes use in preparing for performance and improving their game. It has been proven to help athletes overcome performance anxiety and maintain better focus on game day. I started using visualization when I first began doing contests and competitions as a teenager. The point of visualization is to imagine the ideal. What would it feel like to give an *absolutely perfect* performance? Here's a walk-through of my visualization process.

First, I visualize the space. This is one reason why it can be helpful to visit the venue beforehand. If you are unable to be in the space beforehand, see if you can look up photos of the venue online. Imagine being backstage moments before your performance with the audience waiting expectantly. Visualize stepping out on stage and bowing. Hear the applause. See the space. Is it dark? Can you see faces in the audience? Take time to prepare yourself for the first piece. Savor the anticipation and drama in the room. You are holding every listener in the palm of your hand. Visualize the whole performance in your head, and imagine playing through an absolutely perfect performance. There are absolutely no mistakes. All the most tricky passages—the ones you are always afraid you might mess up—you glide swiftly over with no worries and no problems. After you perform your perfect performance, imagine the thrill and satisfaction you feel as you hear almighty applause. The excitement and energy of the room is overwhelming as you bow and walk offstage!

Your practice session on performance day

On performance day, you should have a light practice session beforehand. Don't wear yourself out, but try to get through everything in your program. Start with some Boot Camp and make sure your fingers are well oiled and warmed up. Go through the most difficult spots, study all the typical places for memory slips, and take a few minutes to play through a spot you most enjoy. But most of all, your performance day practice session should be about mental preparation. I have found that it's not healthy to forbid yourself to get nervous—that never works! Instead, tell yourself that it's absolutely okay to be a little nervous, because you can use that extra energy to make your playing that much better. Another thing to never forbid is making mistakes.

Instead, turn off your "worst critic" by telling yourself that a meaningful performance is more valuable than a mistake-less performance. Assure yourself that no matter how many mistakes crop up, you are capable of getting out of them and transforming them into something beautiful and meaningful. Be confident in what you can do, and get out there and shine.

Review Questions

Question No. 1

How do your practice sessions typically change when preparing for a performance?

Question No. 2

What are the benefits of daily run-throughs as you prepare for performance day?

Question No. 3

What are a few ways you can simulate a performance in the practice room? How might this be helpful to you as you mentally prepare for your performance?

Question No. 4

Take a few minutes to try visualization as a pre-performance strategy. How does this change your perception of your performance? Does it simulate pre-performance jitters? Does it give you more confidence as you visualize success?

≈20≈

Deadlines
Make The World Go Round

"To achieve great things, two things are needed:
a plan, and not quite enough time."

— *Leonard Bernstein*

P racticing isn't always easy for me. Some days are glorious. I feel energized and motivated and my hands seem well-oiled and ready for work. Other days, though, I roll wrong-sidedly out of bed, need more than my usual cups of coffee while my fingers take almost all of forever to warm up. "Wait—how do I play this instrument again?"

But it gets even worse, because some days I not only struggle to remember *how* to play the harp, but I struggle to even *want* to play the harp. I am just plain unmotivated and would rather be doing almost anything else. Have you ever invented chores out of thin air in order to get out of practicing? No? Just me?

It doesn't help either when the outside world can never seem to understand what being a musician is actually like. I can't tell you how many times I've been at social events where I've met a new person and the exchange goes something like this. "So, what do you do?"

"Oh, I play the harp," I say.

"Wow! That's so fun. You're so lucky that you don't have to work for your job. I mean, I wish *I* could just play all day long!"

No matter how many times I've heard this, I always wince just a little bit inside. Because as gratifying as being a musician can be, our vocation requires just as much hard work than any other profession. And if we're being honest, sometimes hard work isn't that fun and finding the motivation to practice is next to impossible.

So far we've had chapters about disciplining yourself to work hard, creating an inviting space to make you work better, and practicing more efficiently so your work gets done faster. But at the end of the day, there are unfortunately still going to be times when practicing feels absolute drudgery. Those days you'll be running on sheer willpower to get anything accomplished at all. You might even feel a little resentment toward your instrument. And this is exactly what deadlines were made for.

Manufactured motivation

The great maestro Leonard Bernstein famously quipped, "To achieve great things, two things are needed: a plan and not quite enough time." Isn't that the truth! Achieving your goal requires detailed planning, hard work and lots of motivation, but often we find motivation lacking. Thankfully though, when our source of motivation runs dry we can have it manufactured. Setting a deadline for yourself (i.e., "not quite enough time") is like a magical key that unlocks the vast treasure trove of motivation. A deadline is a surefire way to give yourself enough motivation to accomplish your goals.

The deadlines you set for yourself can be simple or detailed. For me, the most effective deadlines are the ones that have a little fear attached to them. If I set up a recital at the end of the month and announce my program on Facebook, there's a certain amount of healthy fear involved as I practice. It keeps me motivated to make sure that repertoire is ready in time so I don't make a fool out of myself in front of my audience (like I did in Chapter 18!)

Deadlines come in many forms, and the rise of social media has given us some great options when it comes to setting deadlines. One of my best decisions in life was making a practice log out of my Instagram account. The year after I graduated with my Master's degree from CIM, I took the #100daysofpractice challenge, an idea created by Hilary Hahn that is still trending among classical musicians of Instagram today. The simple explanation of the challenge is to commit to posting a video of yourself practicing to Instagram for one hundred days in a row. I was familiar with my personal need to set deadlines—to regularly set up recitals, performances, and competitions to keep myself accountable—but I had never made *daily* deadlines for myself! I knew every morning that by the end of the day I had to have roughly one minute of something good enough to post for all the world to see. This challenge gave me daily motivation, and I really believe that forcing daily deadlines on myself took my playing to the next level.

Whether it's a competition at the end of the semester, a recital at the end of the month, or a video at the end of the day, give some thought to setting deadlines for yourself. Promise your teacher you'll have the first half of your piece up to tempo for your next lesson. Set up a mock audition and invite your family. Get your friends to come over to hear your piece memorized. Apply for a competition. Commit to a practice challenge on Instagram—anything that will keep you motivated to get things done. Instead of fearing those days of non-motivation and drudgery, anticipate them by giving yourself a little healthy fear. And be encouraged. It's not just you who faces non-motivation. Our whole world is filled with a lack of motivation. Thankfully, deadlines make the world go round.

Review Questions

Question No. 1

Do you ever struggle with non-motivation? When does this typically happen?

Question No. 2

Why are deadlines important for reaching your goals?

Question No. 3

What are two or three deadlines you can create in order to motivate yourself to accomplishing your goals?

≈21≋

You Are The
Instrument

"I should be sorry if I only entertained them.
I wish to make them better."

— *G.F. Handel*

While watching my colleagues perform in their various degree recitals, I made an intriguing observation. An excerpt from a journal entry of mine from college explores this discovery:

May 30, 2016.

Sometimes when I hear a performance at CIM, I try to figure out what I love about the performer as well as what could make the performance even better. Too often, the performance is clean and the music is beautiful—and yet there is a hindrance or barrier, as if the performer is fighting with his instrument to get his ideas across. All the truly great performances have one thing in common: the performers' instruments are one with them. They are united in such a way that it is as if the instrument disappears, and it is just you and the

performer, and an incredible wash of sound in between you and all around you.

I have found this to be true on numerous occasions since. All too often it seems as if we are at war with our instruments, fighting to get this box of wood or tube of brass to do what we want it to do. Too many times the harp for me has seemed to be a barrier to break down rather than a tool. What is the reason for fighting?

I think at a surface level, technique is involved in some way. A complete mastery of technique will be a significant aid in overcoming the hindrance of your instrument. But when I first noticed this in the recital hall at CIM and saw the patterns in dozens of subsequent concerts, my wheels began to turn. What if I thought about it differently? What if it goes deeper than the surface of technique? What if my harp isn't the problem?

What if the instrument is actually *me?*

When you start to think of yourself as the instrument, everything will change. For one thing, it shows you your place. As artists, a big pitfall for us is thinking too much of ourselves and of the importance of our artistic contributions to the world. Our pride can puff

"What if it goes deeper than the surface of technique? What if my harp isn't the problem? What if the instrument is actually me?"

up our heads in such a way that our minds are clouded by unnecessary stress and we aren't able to perform at our best. It affects us in the practice room, too. We can put so much importance on a single performance in our minds that we are laden with worry and frustration when we don't see the progress we want in a practice session. Just as we fight with our instruments to get our ideas across, so we fight with ourselves.

Thinking of yourself as the instrument puts you in your place. But in so doing, it also gives you an immense freedom. It puts you exactly where you need to be. You are not up on a pedestal, you're beside it. You're not on the throne, you're the king's cupbearer. Not master, but servant. When you think of yourself as the instrument, everything changes. You stop thinking about yourself and start thinking about your audience. But in order for this to work, you have to have something to serve. In order to be the instrument, you have to be instrumental for something greater than yourself.

"In order to be the instrument, you have to be instrumental for something greater than yourself."

Why do you do what you do? Why are you pursuing music? Forget all the things clouding your mind and go back to that moment years ago when you first experienced the wonder of it. Your first orchestral concert experience. A Christmas performance at a church in your neighborhood. That time your grandmother sat down at the piano and played in the intimacy of her living room for *just you*. Chances are that moment is directly linked to the reason why you're still pursuing music even now. Why did you choose music? What purpose can you be instrumental in achieving?

For me, my purpose largely has to do with a single word: *beauty*. I have noticed that there is something absolutely beautiful and transcendent in music, and my goal is to communicate that beauty and transcendence as well as I can. It all springs from my Christian faith and my view of God as the source of all true beauty. For me, I think of myself as a simple instrument, meant to communicate beauty to my audience. That not only drives my practice sessions as I hone my craft every day to become a more excellent and useful instrument, but it gives me purpose in a world that is searching for value.

Thinking of myself as the instrument grounds me and gives me something to play for. It puts me in my place while also giving me value and purpose. When I practice and perform this way, the very thing happens to me which I wrote in my journal entry about the instrument. It is as if I, the instrument, disappears. I'm no longer in the way—it's just the audience and the thing I am trying to communicate and the incredible wash of beauty all around.

What about you? What is your greater purpose? Why are you pursuing music and honing your craft? What would you most like to be instrumental in achieving? This idea culminates in a performance but it starts today in the practice room. Stop fighting your instrument. Next time you practice, *be* the instrument and work toward communicating something greater than yourself.

Review Questions

Question No. 1

Have you ever felt that you were fighting with your instrument to get your ideas across? Do you think that this struggle goes deeper than technical ability?

Question No. 2

What are the benefits of thinking of yourself as the instrument? How might this idea free you from fighting with your instrument or yourself?

Question No. 3

In order to think of yourself as the instrument, you have to be instrumental for something greater than yourself. This goes back to the first chapter on finding your purpose. Take a minute to reflect: what is your purpose? Why you are pursuing music? In what ways can you be instrumental towards fulfilling your greater purpose?

Question No. 4

Take a moment to reflect on why you started pursuing music in the first place. Is that moment linked to your greater purpose in any way?

≈ 22 ≈

To Be Exemplary,
Learn By Example

*"If I have seen further it is by standing
on the shoulders of giants."*

— *Isaac Newton*

D o you have any role models? Ludwig van Beethoven did. He idolized the great Wolfgang
Amadeus Mozart—copying his scores, basing
his own compositions off of Mozart's symphonies, and
studying his music avidly. It is purported that Beethoven often dreamed of studying with Mozart growing up.
One 19th-century biographer gives an account in which
Beethoven's dream comes true—after many years of
careful study, practice, and performance, he meets Mozart face-to-face and plays for him. There is only a single
source for this tale, but supposedly Beethoven played
a showpiece for Mozart, who responded rather coldly
to his performance. Desperate to please his idol, Beethoven asked him to hum a theme on which to base an
improvisation. Mozart's attention was riveted at once

as he watched Beethoven turn his theme into a brilliant masterpiece, and as he finished Mozart was said to have turned aside to the rest of Beethoven's audience and declared, "Mark that young man; he will make himself a name in the world!" And make a name he did.

Whether or not the story itself is true, the idea behind the tale is as real as Beethoven's own existence. Beethoven looked up to Mozart, studied him, copied his patterns, steeped himself in his compositional style. And it wasn't just Mozart who he admired—he also looked up to Josef Haydn (with whom he did end up studying for a period). Both of these men were undeniably influential to Beethoven as he studied composition, the mechanics of music, and how to create his own unique style which eventually turned into the masterpieces we know and love—the masterpieces that inevitably swept the world off its feet.

The importance of a role model

Beethoven made a name for himself—he is now considered to be the most exemplary of history's composers. Have you ever wondered how Beethoven came to be exemplary? He learned by example. The greatest artists are never just "born that way;" rather, *that way* is learned. A composer achieves mastery because he has first studied the masters. A novelist is notable because she has first read the noteworthy. A songwriter's lyrics sing because he has first listened to the greatest songs. To be exemplary, you must first learn by example. In your journey as a musician, give yourself the gift of looking up to a few worthy role models. If you let yourself learn, study, and steep in the methods of a few great artists, their influence could in turn make you influential. Their example could make you exemplary.

Invest in a private teacher

If you are an amateur, student, or non-professional, the first role model you should be searching for is a teacher. I cannot stress this enough: If you are serious about getting better at your instrument, get a private teacher who will invest in you. No amount of DIY, YouTube tutorials, half-hearted tutors, or help from friends will surpass the immeasurable value of a private teacher who cares about you, challenges you, guides you, critiques you, and ultimately forms you. There is no way to measure just how beneficial this could be to you in your musical journey.

What makes a good teacher? When searching for a good musical instructor, keep these things in mind:

Good teachers take their craft seriously. They are passionate about what they do. A good teacher has mastered their art through ten thousand hours of practice—and then ten thousand more. They are motivated to propagate what they have learned about their art because they love it, and it is worthy of being passed down.

Good teachers have role models themselves. If you are interviewing a new teacher for private lessons, it's not a bad idea to casually ask them who they consider to be the greatest at their instrument. This will give you an idea of the types of people they look up to and respect. A good teacher is humble enough to learn from outside sources and look to even greater artists for feedback.

Good teachers care about you. They're not in it for the money. They genuinely care about your well being and your improvement—not only as a musician but as a person, too. They will watch closely to make sure you are perfecting your technique so that you don't injure yourself. They will be sure that they don't give you a piece that is too difficult for you so that you learn at the right pace without becoming frustrated or giving up. They will be observant if you seem a little more tired or stressed than usual and ask if you are okay. Good teachers care about you—they pursue a relationship that goes deeper than the notes on the page.

Good teachers push you further than you thought possible. Because they care about you, good teachers will expect great things from you. A teacher with low expectations is one who doesn't seem to think you're worth it—and you *are* worth it, so if your teacher doesn't expect a lot from you, get a different teacher. Good teachers challenge you and push you to achieve the next level of playing.

Good teachers invest in you. A good teacher won't wave goodbye at the end of your lesson and never give you a moment's thought until the following week. They will invest in you by creating lesson plans, hand-picking curriculum or repertoire that fits you, and spending time outside of your lessons in hopes that you grow and succeed. If you are looking toward being a professional musician, a good teacher will give you all the resources you need to pursue that career: They will give you their honest advice. They will help you apply and prepare for competitions, colleges, and scholarships. They will provide recommendation letters and give you advice on next steps. Most of all, they will give you performance opportunities and prepare you for anything that might come your way.

"Good teachers care about you. They're not in it for the money. They genuinely care about your well being and your improvement."

If you find a teacher that fits the descriptions above, respect them. Listen to what they say and work hard to accomplish what they ask. Be open with them and communicate how your practice time went. What went well? What did you struggle with? Tell them if you don't understand something. If they set weekly goals for you, practice enough in the week to accomplish them by your next lesson. If they point out errors in your technique, respect them enough to fix those problems. It is a rare thing to find a teacher who cares about you, challenges you, and invests in you that much—if you have such a teacher, you are blessed. A teacher like that respects you by giving you considerably more than what they charge. Give them the basic respect they deserve by following their example and instruction.

Find other role models too

Perhaps you are like me: a professional who doesn't regularly study with a private teacher anymore. But just because you're out of school and graduated to "professional" doesn't mean that you can stop learning. In fact, your learning has only just begun! It doesn't matter if you are an amateur or a professional. Wherever you are in your journey, it is always essential that you choose a few people for role models. A good starting point is to hand-pick four different types of role models: a superstar, a professional, a teacher/mentor, and a non-musician.

The first role model should be a superstar who inspires you to dream big. Pick one famous musician who you think is spectacular. He or she doesn't have to play your instrument—the idea is to study someone who has been very successful as a musician. Study their music, study their methods, their outlook on life, their practice techniques. Dream of being as great as them one day.

The second role model is a professional musician who can motivate you. Look for a successful and outstanding musician, but not necessarily a celebrity. Someone you can look up to not because they're popular, but because they inspire you. Social media is filled with people like this who are honing their craft every day and inspiring other musicians online. Follow one or two people who will inspire you to keep going and stay motivated.

The third role model should be your private teacher who will challenge you. If you are a professional and don't have a teacher anymore, you should still have a mentor—someone you respect who can give you guidance and help you grow. Maybe this is a former teacher or an older, wiser musician with whom you can become close and form a bond. Whoever it is, they should care about you enough to challenge you and push you to the next level.

Your last role model should be a non-musician who gives you focus and perspective. Find someone who doesn't have anything to do with music who you admire and respect because of their life purpose. You could admire them because of their faith, their drive, their business sense, or what they have contributed to their world. For example, my mom isn't a musician but she will always be one of my biggest role models because she embodies the perfect combination of diligence, patience, and sacrificial love. This type of role model gets you out of your musical box and provides a different perspective on you—not as a *musician*, but as a *person*—that can influence you in big ways.

As you have learned by example, lead by example.

As you seek these mentors and role models, don't forget to take the next step and become a mentor yourself. There are always people who are seeking to grow and learn, and you have knowledge, experience, and wisdom to offer. Be willing to share your knowledge with them. This doesn't mean you have to immediately offer private lessons or become an elementary school teacher. But it does mean that you should hold that knowledge in your hands loosely and be willing to share what has been given you. As you have been influenced, be an influencer—as you have learned by example, lead by example. This is the beautiful moment when the "exemplary" trait is passed down to the next generation: just as Mozart was an example to Beethoven, Beethoven became an example to the rest of the world. And just as your role models will influence you, so you should influence the role models of the future. In order to be exemplary, learn by example. And then lead by example to make a difference.

Review Questions

Question No. 1

Why is it important to have a private teacher?

Question No. 2

Do you have a mentor, role model, or teacher? What are some ways you can better respect and learn from them?

Question No. 3

What are the four types of role models you should have? Who would you choose as your four role models?

≈23≈

Become A
Submarine

*"Hardships often prepare ordinary people
for an extraordinary destiny."*

— *C.S. Lewis*

I t's difficult to say what is the most valuable lesson
I learned from my teacher and mentor, Yolanda
Kondonassis, during my time under her care at the
Cleveland Institute of Music. I could choose hundreds,
thousands even, of valuable tidbits, life lessons, and
words of advice given me in those precious and eagerly
anticipated Tuesday lessons.

Perhaps the lessons in which I learned the most
were the ones in which I did less playing. As a harpist
at a major conservatory working towards an accelerat-
ed performance program, a eurhythmics minor, prep-
ping for major competitions, leading a Bible study on
the side, and tutoring up to dozens of conservatory students every week to pay bills, sometimes I came to my
lessons just plain exhausted. I remember on more than

one of these occasions Ms. Kondonassis encouraged me to excel in all these areas by mastering the art of compartmentalization—to become a submarine.

> *"I build [compartments] around the things that matter most to me, just like the sections of a submarine. If one leaks, the damage is contained and won't flood the whole vessel. I've used this system for decades and it's proven to be a lifesaver – not to mention a sanity-saver. I will wager to say that there are few careers more demanding than a life in the arts, and even fewer still that require more ongoing practice, maintenance, time, and compartment-building to assure quality control, than a life in classical music performance."*

As helpful as becoming a submarine sounded, it was easier said than done! I especially struggled with this as an eager and passionate young student who wanted to do her best at everything. It's hard to not let a disappointing grade on an exam, troubling news from back home, or the 15,879 other things on your to-do list bleed into your thoughts during a practice session. These have the potential to not only make your practice time completely unfocused and distracting, but when you do eventually get around to practicing, they can actually affect the expression and phrasing of your repertoire! I remember on a few of the most stressful weeks I'd come into my lessons and Ms. Kondonassis would say, "It's really good, but this part should sound triumphant. It seems kind of mournful today." Or, "This passage should be as delicate as lace, but it's just a little bit strained." It is easy to let the stresses of everyday life affect the way we practice, and consequently, the way we perform. But Ms. Kondonassis recognizes this as unhelpful and even unhealthy. "We cannot be thinking about everything in our lives at once," she says. Practicing can be a calm and comforting haven if we train ourselves to free our minds from stresses and concerns in the practice room. Here are some thoughts that have been inspired by Ms. Kondonassis on healthy submarining in the midst of stressful times:

Reserve practice time for practice. It takes discipline, but reserving a segment of your day to dedicated practicing works wonders. Most of the time, those stressful thoughts can wait an hour or two. Won't you feel better by working through a satisfying practice session and crossing that off your list? One trick I have learned during especially stressful days is to make really specific goals and set a timer for less than you think you need. This will force your brain to work quickly and keep those nagging, stressful thoughts at bay.

Set aside special time for thought processing. Reserving practice time for practice doesn't mean you should never process what is happening in your life. Grant yourself some dedicated time for processing and sorting through your thoughts. It also can give you more incentive to not think about your stresses during practice time. "Yes, I'm stressed about that, but it can wait until tonight." Acknowledge how you feel, but tell yourself you can think about it all you want later.

No matter how busy you may be, taking just a few minutes before bed to do a quick recap of the day, sort through thoughts and feelings, journal, and plan your next day can be incredibly beneficial. I especially recommend journaling. It's a wonderful release to be able to flesh out and physically see all your thoughts on paper—and sometimes once you write everything down things don't seem so bad. Another great reason to keep a journal is so you can look back on all the stressful days you survived and see how much you've grown since then.

However you choose to do it, set aside a few moments each day to be alone with your thoughts. In this day and age it seems people are spending less and less time dedicated to silent thought. But try it for a few weeks and you might just find that you are pretty good company for yourself!

"Just remember, you're not a machine." Alice Chalifoux, the great harp pioneer and pedagogue, was known to say this to her students during their most frazzled lessons. At the end of the day, you are in fact still human. Sometimes it's appropriate and even necessary to take time off, refuel, and focus on things more important than your instrument. And sometimes (I talk about this more in Chapter 26) your thoughts and feelings are just what is needed to season your playing with a special meaning that is unique to you.

Ms. Kondonassis describes compartmentalization as beneficial both for the music and for yourself. "We have to be clear enough to focus on the heart of the music, the physical feeling, the character, the series of steps required, and the solitary task of creating something unique. This type of practice is not only good for the music, but is very beneficial for overall mental health." Take her advice and become a submarine. Explore the benefits of compartmentalization. Learn the discipline of sealing off your practice time away from unnecessary stresses and worries, allowing in only the ones that truly matter. And no matter how stormy your day might be, if your compartments hold up, your vessel will stay its course.

Review Questions

Question No. 1

What are the benefits of compartmentalization?

Question No. 2

What are the different "compartments" in your life?

Question No. 3

What kinds of stresses and concerns typically enter your practice session with you?

Question No. 4

What kinds of activities might help you process stress and worry?

≋ 24 ≋

You Are Worth More Than
Your Practice Session

"May your work be in keeping with your purpose."

— *Leonardo da Vinci*

W hy am I here? Should I even be pursuing music? Am I wasting my time? Am I good enough? I circled around the halls of my music conservatory basement. It was a cacophony of noise as a hundred different students practiced diligently, but amongst the noise these silent questions whispered through a hundred different practice room walls. Every question ultimately boiled down to this: "Who am I, really? And whoever I am, am I enough?" It was the biggest insecurity of the students studying at the Cleveland Institute of Music—the questions every one of us asked at some time or another, and the enemy that threatened every day to steal our joy and our productivity and leave us empty and searching and lost.

I was used to hearing questions of identity amongst my friends back home as we grew into adults and began to own new responsibilities, but when I first arrived at CIM it shocked me that *these* students would struggle with these questions of being "enough"—good enough, valuable enough, worthy enough. I watched in disbelief as they questioned their careers, questioned who they really are at their core. "*These* students struggle with this?" I thought. "The ones who were accepted by audition to a major conservatory, who are studying with world-renowned teachers?" In my mind they had already proven their worth. But then I took a closer look, and what I saw was a mirror image of myself.

As it turns out, freshman Rachel struggled with insecurities, too. I left my Virginia town with no idea of what to expect in college—I didn't personally know a single soul in Cleveland. Before I moved to Cleveland, I remember realizing one day that I would have to perform recitals on campus, and my fearful response surprised me. I grew up in a small city where there were many classical music lovers, but rarely any who knew the harp repertoire and could critique it. The thought of giving a recital for consummate performers or renowned professors or talented classmates excited me—but it terrified me, too. And once I arrived at CIM for orientation week, it didn't get better. I became even more insecure when I heard the students chattering around me, referring to string quartets by their opus numbers and dropping names of composers like Bruckner and Webern and Khachaturian—names I had never heard in my life!

"I don't know a single thing about classical music!" I realized. And that ignorance frightened me.

The two big questions

Why do we struggle with insecure thoughts? Why do we battle questions of identity and worth? We know on the surface that these thoughts can be unhealthy, yet we can't avoid them. We wonder what our identity really is, and then we wonder if who we are at our core is valuable enough to be worth the amount of space we take up in this world. Every insecure thought boils down to these two big questions. The first is, "Who am I, really?" And the second is, "Am I really enough?"

If you were at a dinner party and a stranger asked you to describe yourself, what would you say? What would you default to? "I'm a harpist," I might say, or "I'm a music lover, bibliophile, and hiker." But is that really true? Is "harpist" or "music lover" or "bibliophile" or "hiker" really *who I am* at my core? These are all things I do for a living or enjoy in spare time, but if I think about it, none of those things are actually *me*. These days I'm hearing a lot of talk about different groups we can categorize ourselves in and identify with: Democrat or Republican, musician or engineer, INFJ or ENTP. And some of this is okay. There is nothing wrong with finding community among people who are like you and in whom you share beliefs or personality or commonality. But community is different than categorization. Community is something you *find*, but categorization is something you *do*. To categorize others is to place them in a box that keeps them from realizing their true potential. I would venture to say that our society has gone a little overboard with categorization. Why? Because in so doing, we teach ourselves that who we really *are* has to do with the categories we place ourselves in. Finding identity only in things that describe you will limit you and hinder you from being who you truly are.

So if I am not a harpist, music lover, bibliophile, or hiker, who am I? If you are not defined by your instrument or your career or your personality, who are you? *Who are we, really?* The answer lies deep in our DNA, rooted in the beginning of time: *I am a unique human being, placed on this earth for a unique purpose.* This statement is packed with some valuable insight as to who you really are. First, you are *unique*:

> "*If you are not defined by your instrument or your career or your personality, who are you? Who are we, really?*"

There isn't anyone like you. Scientists and theorists may be able to categorize you loosely into a personality type or statistic, but really there isn't anyone with exactly the same makeup as you have. Your fingerprints and DNA demonstrate this! You are unique, but you are also a *human being.* Your uniqueness distinguishes you from everything else, but your humanness unites you to every other human on this planet. And that humanness gives you immense value. As a human being with immense value, you have been placed here for *a unique purpose.* You have talents and gifts and an approach to life that is distinct from anyone else. You have a purpose to fulfill that gives you incalculable worth.

With that definition of who you are, does that make you enough? Surprisingly, the answer is no. In order to have a healthy view of ourselves, we must first realize that at the end of the day *we aren't enough.* None of us are. As much as we try to reach perfection, we will never quite get there. There will always be someone better than we are. There will always be something we can do better, something more we can achieve, something more we can be. No matter how hard we try, if the standard is perfection we will always fall short. It doesn't help to lie to yourself about being the best or the most good-looking or the smartest or the most talented—because deep down, you really know that none of that is really true. Is this realization depressing? It doesn't have to be. What if this realization was actually freeing? What if there was a way to realize that in yourself you *aren't* enough but you are still immensely valuable?

My whole outlook on life is centered around this idea. *I am not enough*—I fail to achieve perfection every day—but that doesn't affect my intrinsic *value.* I have value not because of what I do but because of what my identity is rooted in. If you were to ask me what my identity is, I would tell you it was rooted in my Christian faith. It's not rooted in a categorization of beliefs or doctrines, but in what I've found the Bible to boil down to: measuring up is hopeless, but the God of the Bible chooses to give value and worth to humans anyway. This perspective of innate worth has rooted me and grounded me more than anything else, giving me purpose in a confusing world.

Identity in practice

How do we make these big questions relevant in the practice room? Here are some practical steps.

Realize that you have value, with or without your instrument. Your music or talent or success or career doesn't define you, much less your practice session! You have value without anything added on. Let this realization give you dignity and motivate you to be the best you can be—out of gratitude and generosity, not out of fear.

Be encouraged, not frustrated. It can be easy to become frustrated in a practice room because of insecurities. Frustration in yourself or your playing is a type of narcissism. Get rid of these thoughts by being honest with yourself. You *aren't* as good or diligent or smart or talented as your potential. You can be, though. As you work hard and pursue excellence, you can reach higher levels of perfection and higher levels of potential. That is why this realization should encourage rather than frustrate you.

Never compare yourself to others unless it is constructive. Unhealthy comparison says that other people are better than you, so you might as well not try. It becomes jealous and is rooted in selfishness. It wishes that the other person wasn't as successful as you. Healthy comparison rejoices in the successes and talents of another person and seeks to learn and grow from their journey. Those who compare themselves in a healthy manner do not beat down the one enjoying success, and they don't beat themselves down, either. As Elizabeth Gaskell said, "We can praise the one without hitting at the other."

Look beyond comparison to something more valuable. There are so many worthy things for you to concentrate on! The music itself that you are learning is worth more of your attention. Simone Dinnerstein says we should more often compare ourselves to our music than to others. "I think that the more you can concentrate on the music itself, and unlocking the interpretation of it, the better. It takes the focus off of ourselves and places it on to the music. Then the challenges and frustrations are between the music and our own abilities to bring it to life, as opposed to thinking about how other people handle those challenges."

My freshman year at CIM was transformative because I spent a lot of time analyzing and processing my own identity. I came to better understand that I didn't have worth or value because I knew certain facts, or looked a certain way, or practiced enough, or impressed my professors. My value was rooted in something greater than that. Each of us have value because we are unique human beings, placed on this earth for a unique purpose. That value is innate, with or without our instruments in hand. Next time you enter your practice room, realize that your practice session, your instrument, and even your career don't define you. The world is worth more than your practice session, and so are you.

Review Questions

Question No. 1

What are the typical insecure questions you ask yourself? How does your greater purpose speak into those insecurities?

Question No. 2

If your identity is not defined by the activities that you do or the instrument that you play, who are you? What is your identity?

Question No. 3

Many of us struggle with the question of "Am I enough?" How can an answer of "no" to this question be freeing rather than depressing?

Question No. 4

What are some ways that a proper view of your identity can inform your practice sessions?

≈ 25 ≈

End On A
High Note

"Keep your face to the sunshine and you cannot see a shadow."

— *Helen Keller*

I f anyone finds himself a weary traveler in a dark forest, let him climb a tree. But not just any tree. Let him look for the tallest tree of the forest. Its ancient trunk towers valiantly upward, and its branches spread shade far and wide across the vast, unending woodlands. It is important to select *this* tree. Only a worthy tree should be climbed, and only a worthy climber should attempt it. He must possess both courage and tenacity. A worthy climber is not afraid to brave the danger and exert the effort necessary to reach the top. But he is also tenacious. When climbing becomes even more difficult and frustrating than he ever thought possible, he remains hopeful, holds on tightly, and finally reaches the top. As the traveler sits on the treetops, all his weariness is forgotten. He can see the whole forest at a single glance. He catches a glimpse of the edge of the forest to the east where he started, far away in the distance. And he sees ahead the forest's opening to his homeland in the west, not so very far away. The traveler is heartened by how far he has come, and the encouragement motivates him to travel the last few miles home.

Climb high

An intense practice session is often frustrating, especially when you have a goal you feel is very difficult to reach. Most of the chapters thus far will help you with days like these, but even if you are still feeling frustrated, it is best to maintain a positive attitude. As the traveler climbed a tree to see the whole view of the forest, so should you combine courage with tenacity to achieve small successes in your journey. Choose a tree to climb so that you may be encouraged by how far you've come.

On your most frustrating practice days, end on a high note by keeping these things in mind.

Don't become weary from failure. Teach yourself to view failure as a step forward, not a step back. Remember, a practice haven is a very safe place to fail! Use failure to get to know yourself. What are your common pitfalls? Why do you make the mistakes you tend to make? What can you learn from your so-called failures in order to get better, hone your craft, and step up your game? Don't just get frustrated and angry with yourself when you fail, because frustration solves nothing, creates an atmosphere that inhibits learning, and is actually a type of harmful self-focus. Instead, view failure as an opportunity to grow.

Get out your practice journal. What could have gone better today? If you analyze your weakest points in order use them to your advantage, you will cultivate a haven where productivity and growth can thrive. You should use your practice journal to analyze your strengths, too. What did you do well that day? What were you really satisfied with? What are you proud of? What are your success stories? Sometimes we tend to get too critical and bear down a little too hard on ourselves. Being able to write these things down in a journal is a wonderful way of tracking your success. One of my favorite things to do is to look back on previous journal entries—to read that in October I was struggling with a particular technique issue, and to suddenly realize now that I haven't struggled with that issue in months! Journaling is an encouraging pastime because you can see in ink how far you've come.

Make realistic goals. As you journal through frustrating days, make sure you write down different types of goals to check off. You should certainly write down ambitious goals for the day. But even if you don't accomplish your biggest goal, you should be able to check off a few other things in your practice journal—like warming up, focusing on a technique problem, or practicing with the #3xperfectly rule. Even if a practice session is grueling and frustrating, you will be able to find some satisfaction in a mostly checked-off journal entry.

Sometimes frustration is heightened with stress. If you have a performance coming up soon, be aware of any stress that might hinder your practice time. Being frustrated with your progress won't help you learn the notes in time, but calming yourself with some slow, methodical Boot Camp will be one of the best ways to combat pre-performance anxiety.

"Isn't it nice to think that tomorrow is a new day with no mistakes in it yet?"

—Anne of Green Gables

End on a high note. No matter how frustrating a practice session, end with something that is satisfying and doable for you. Bring the tempo back down and play the passage. Go back to a section of the piece you can already play well and enjoy. Or just mess around and improvise your favorite melody for fun! Ending on a high note will make you want to come back and keep meeting your goals.

Tomorrow is a new day

Even in your most frustrating practice session, remember that there is always tomorrow. As Anne of Green Gables said, "Isn't it nice to think that tomorrow is a new day with no mistakes in it yet?" Maybe perfection can never be *completely* achieved, but the potential for perfection tomorrow is always new. You may not be able to meet every goal, learn all the notes, or phrase your music perfectly today, but there will be more days to to pursue higher versions of perfection in your playing. Give yourself some grace and let yourself steep in the music a little bit. Remember that taking things slowly always proves to be better in the long run. Remember that any amount of success in a practice session makes it a successful practice session. And remember that, even if you don't nail a passage today, with hard work and some positivity you will be able to slowly climb upward, branch by branch, until you reach the top. No matter what happens in a practice session, you can end it on a high note by reminding yourself that, like a tree whose roots run deep and spread far, growth isn't always seen.

Review Questions

Question No. 1

Why is positivity important while practicing? Why might it be helpful to end a practice session on a high note?

Question No. 2

What are some ways that failure can be a positive, rather than negative, experience?

Question No. 3

What are some reasons why keeping a practice journal can be an encouragement to your practice time?

≈26≈

Don't Forget To Live

"Why hurry over beautiful things?
Why not linger and enjoy them?"

— *Clara Schumann*

Freshman year at CIM, I found myself in one of my very first lessons with my new harp teacher. I admit I was still in disbelief that this harp celebrity, Yolanda Kondonassis, was now *my* harp teacher. This harp giant, the one I had looked up to all these years, the one whose albums I had been listening to on repeat for almost a decade, was sitting right beside me and listening to me play? I must be dreaming!

I was learning Salzedo's *Variations on a Theme in Ancient Style*, a technical showpiece, and in that particular lesson I played Variation 5, "Chords & Fluxes." The variation starts with "Chords," a loud, boisterous, confident beginning. Suddenly, it switches to a series of very fast but delicate arpeggios, the "Fluxes," that travel up and down the instrument. The switch is tricky and the arpeggios are difficult to make even, so I was focusing on maintaining good technique as I plowed through the passage. I thought I had played it pretty well — it sounded even to me and it was well executed. But when Ms. Kondonassis stopped me, her words were surprising.

"I wish I could have taken you to the lace factory I visited with my daughter last week," she said. Yolanda Kondonassis wished she could've taken *me* to the lace factory she visited with her daughter? I tried to keep my mouth from dropping. "I would have loved for you to have seen that room full of lace! I wish you could have run your hands over some and experienced for yourself how delicate, how detailed, how exquisite it felt. Then you would know exactly how to play this passage. It should sound like the way lace feels."

I was amazed. Most teachers would have told me how to change my technique to get the right sound. But she was interested in giving me an experience that might help me actually make the music tangible. I closed my eyes—I had experience with fabric. My grandmother taught me how to sew when I was ten years old. I had run my hands over countless variations on a theme of

> *"Most teachers would have told me how to change my technique to get the right sound. But she was interested in giving me an experience that might help me actually make the music tangible."*

lace. The "fluxes" in this section were like a bolt of elegant lace—one single piece of fabric as a whole, but a never-ending treasury of intricate designs up close. I played the variation again with a new perspective. The mood of the whole passage changed completely. And for the rest of my life, I don't think I'll ever play that passage of the *Variations* again without thinking about a room full of lace.

Experiences shape us

Our minds are designed to store powerful memories that leave imprints on our lives. Whether it's a momentous memory like graduating from college, or a tiny, seemingly insignificant one like running a hand over lace, experiences have the potential to impact us in powerful ways. I have learned that as I seek to become a more perfected player, the experiences that have shaped me show up in my playing every day. My memories are a powerful asset to my development as an artist! They mean I have something genuinely unique to offer.

I remember reading a story years ago about a wise old musician who went to hear a violin prodigy perform Massenet's *Meditation from "Thais."* When asked what he thought of the performance, the old musician said, "She is a very good violinist. But she is young. She will never be ready to play this piece until she has learned of love and heartbreak. Then—then she will be truly great."

Maturity comes through living

I learned this for myself the very last week of my conservatory experience. My recital was a week away, the only thing between me and my Master's degree. My preparation was going well, better than all my other degree recitals, and I felt that with a week of practicing I should be ready. But that was all put on hold when suddenly in the middle of the night, my brother Justin (also a student at CIM) woke me up. He was in excruciating pain.

"You have to take me to the hospital," he said.

As it turned out, Justin had a rare condition called Rhabdomyolysis. This condition can develop in athletes and weight lifters, causing unbelievable muscle pain due to rupturing cells in the muscle tissue, ultimately resulting in kidney damage—and in worst cases, organ failure and death. Thankfully he was treated in time to make a full recovery, but in the night we spent in the emergency room and the weeks that followed, I watched my brother bravely endure more pain than I ever had witnessed before. It is a sobering thing to watch someone you love suffer beside you, and not be able to do anything to help. I was just thankful to have been there for him and eventually be assured that he would recover. It really put into perspective the things that are the most important in life, and it gave me a newfound respect for my brother's courage amidst unimaginable pain.

Needless to say, I didn't get in as much practice time that week as I had originally planned. I spent much of that time in the hospital that week. But I was right where I needed to be. I gave my recital, inscribing in the program a dedication to my brother, *"the strongest man I know."* And I like to think my performance that night was more seasoned, more mature, more contemplative, and more grateful because of the priceless lessons I had learned that week about the preciousness of life and courage in the face of adversity.

Music becomes tangible when you draw from the most momentous, insignificant, poignant, tender, sorrowful, hilarious, frightening, angering, and victorious moments in your life. You don't find those in a practice room. So don't forget to step away from your instrument every now and then to live.

Review Questions

Question No. 1

According to this chapter, what is the secret to mature musicianship?

Question No. 2

What are some reasons why gaining life experience can make you a better musician?

Question No. 3

Have you ever connected a piece of music to an experience that happened to you? How did this shape your performance?

Follow Rachel on Social Media:

 @RachelLeeHall

 @RachelHallHarp

 @RachelLeeHall

Printed in Great Britain
by Amazon

26753695R00096